Cultural Politics - Queer Reading

Cultural Politics -
Queer Reading

Alan Sinfield

London

Permission to reprint portions of W.H. Auden's "The Truest Poetry Is the Most Feigning" is granted by Faber and Faber Ltd. and Random House, Inc. From *Collected Shorter Poems 1927–1957* (London: Faber and Faber, 1966). Copyright © 1966 by W.H. Auden.

Simultaneously published 1994 by Routledge, 11 New Fetter Lane, London EC4P 4EE and the University of Pennsylvania Press, 418 Service Drive, Philadelphia, PA 19104

British Library Cataloguing in Publication Data

A catalogue record for this book is available from the British Library

ISBN 0-415-10947-7
    0-415-10948-5 (pbk)

Contents

Foreword

Until quite recently, "doing English Literature" meant joining the flow of an established tradition of wisdom and beauty. One might divert into "American Literature," or even "Commonwealth Literature," but these were considered largely to be tributaries. When "Black Literature" and "Women's Literature" forced their way to the surface, some people regarded them also as wayward eddies to be evaluated in terms of their contribution to the mainstream; it was upon that assumption that new directions were tolerated.

That phase did not last long: subordinated groups began to resist the privileging of the traditional canon and to assert the validity of their own cultures. The significance of such moves may be estimated from the hostility they provoked. In the United States, college courses that recognized the diversity of U.S. people were mocked. William Bennett, Secretary of State for Education in the Reagan administration, stated openly the political reason for reasserting tradition: it enshrines "American" values. "Our society was founded upon such principles as justice, liberty, government with the consent of the governed, and equality under the law" (well, male homosexuality is indeed equally illegal in half of the states). These ideas, Bennett says, "descended directly from great epochs of Western civilization," and they "are the glue that binds together our pluralistic nation."[1] Bennett acknowledges there the political role of mainstream culture: it suppresses differences. For subcultures may be power bases—points at which alternative or oppositional ideologies may achieve plausibility. And that may be bad for the state and bad for a capitalist economy. Those are the issues for E.D. Hirsch, Jr., who believes that U.S. people must be taught a hegemonic idea of "America," in order to hold off "cultural fragmentation, civil antagonism, illiteracy, and economic-technological ineffectualness."[2]

In the United Kingdom, in 1991, Prince Charles lamented "a general flight from our great literary heritage." But whose heritage is it? He finds *Henry V* a helpful guide to the demands made upon princes (perhaps anticipating enterprises grander than have so far befallen him); emboldened by this personal link with the bard, he infers that Shakespeare's "roots are ours, his language is ours, his culture ours."[3] Of course, this is not true for all British people; the assumption that it should be effects a pressure towards conformity.

The U.K. Government is not one to miss a chance for ideological reinforcement. Observing that teaching methods which respect the students' experience may develop the imaginative potential of non-privileged students, and hence lead them to expect jobs and a decent lifestyle, it has introduced compulsory Shakespeare tests for fourteen-year-olds.

> Mercutio [who is dying] refers to himself as "a grave man." What *two* meanings does he expect the listeners to understand?[4]

That is the entire question on the examination paper: two lines are allocated in the answer book for each "meaning," with no space for saying how they might relate to each other. Now, I can envisage arguments that this is not, after all, one of the drearier lines in *Romeo and Juliet*. Perhaps a poor pun is a sign of Mercutio's failing powers. But these candidates are not invited to consider any of that; just to know that there may be two meanings to "grave" in this instance, and implicitly—stupidly—to admire. For that kind of thing, working-class, African, and Asian Britons are expected to forsake their subcultures. And while they are spending time working through a whole play in anticipation of such questions, they cannot be learning skills and knowledges that might give them a worthwhile insight into the world they are inheriting.

Culture is political. That is the key axiom of *cultural materialism*— Raymond Williams's term for analytic work which sees texts as inseparable from the conditions of their production and reception in history; as involved, necessarily, in the making of meanings which are always, finally, political meanings. Literary writing, like all cultural production, operates through an appeal for recognition: "The world is like *this*, isn't it?" it says in effect; and that has to be political. We make sense of ourselves and our situations within an ongoing contest of representations, and they come vested with varying degrees of authority. Some are endorsed by secretaries of state, professors, princes, and examination boards; to assert a subcultural framework of interpretation in the face of such ideological power, you need a good deal of self-assurance. "When someone with the authority of a teacher describes the world and you are not in it"—when your subculture is not acknowledged—"there is a moment of psychic disequilibrium, as if you looked into a mirror and saw nothing," Adrienne Rich says. "It takes some strength of soul—and not just individual strength, but collective understanding—to resist this void, this nonbeing, into which you are thrust, and to stand up, demanding to be seen and heard."5 To develop that "collective understanding" is a project for cultural materialists.

Simply to set aside mainstream culture would be to leave much of its power unchallenged. This book, as a whole and in each of its chapters, starts from mainstream texts and assumptions and moves toward subcultural readings and the principles that might inform them. Jane Austen's *Persuasion* is considered in terms of how South Asian women might read it; Shakespeare's *Venus and Adonis* from the viewpoint of gay men. Writers such as Christopher Marlowe, Walt Whitman, Tennessee Williams, Audre Lorde, and Thom Gunn have been accommodated in the mainstream, but awkwardly: I dwell upon this to show the scope for subcultural reading formations. In the first chapter, I set typically liberal readings of *The Merchant of Venice* against left- and right-wing versions, in the course of engaging the largely taboo topic of how Jewish people might cope with such a text. Other subordinated groups may handle Shakespearean authority in other ways. Can he be claimed as a gay author?—the question was raised, in 1992–93, in the English popular press. I assess in what sense it might be answered.

It is sometimes said that cultural materialists place everyone else historically but leave their own formation unanalyzed. I find this allegation hard to comprehend; so much of what I, at least, have written seems almost self-regardingly preoccupied with the history of the U.K. left. Chapter two should be explicit enough: here I attempt a historical analysis of the conditions in which cultural materialism emerged, distinguishing its approach to art from others in the Marxist tradition (Herbert Marcuse, Louis Althusser). Again, the argument tilts toward sexual politics: "effeminacy" is discovered to have structured, and fractured, conventional Englit. In chapter three, the mainstream Freudian ideology of the Cold War is studied as a context for the most successful U.S. dramatist, Tennessee Williams; yet it is found to have provoked a destabilization that derived from the gayness it was exploiting. Nonetheless, it is a question how far we can deduce a specifically dissident dramatic mode from Williams's work, or from that of present-day lesbian performance artists. Chapter four starts from an assertion of the right of mainstream Englit to the true interpretation of a poem by W.H. Auden. To counter this position, I elaborate a theory of subcultural reading, and a role for lesbian and gay intellectuals that is "beyond Englit." Thom Gunn's poems about AIDS are adduced as a test case. Yet the recuperative manipulations of mainstream culture may be observed in relation to Gunn's work, and that of Jeanette Winterson.

The dash in my title, therefore—*Cultural Politics - Queer Reading*—is not a slash, not a period, not a colon, not a comma, not a hyphen, not an arrow. It figures a break which is also a link, and a movement across. Cultural politics comprises, advances toward, and is redirected by subcultural reading.

Male gayness runs through these discussions because it is part of my argument that intellectuals should work in their own subcultural constituencies. Also, literature and gayness intrude peculiarly upon each other; and, at the time of writing, the most exciting ideas in cultural politics are being developed in lesbian and gay studies. Further and conversely (a lot of the argument seems to come out like that), many sexual dissidents are having a bad time at the moment, despite the success of lesbian and gay studies in the United States (success may also, of course, be incorporation). If Silence = Death, writing may be a positive contribution.

At the same time, I have tried to maintain a steady awareness of other subcultures—having learnt a good deal from them. In Europe, lesbian and gay activism is virtually unthinkable outside the assumption of a broad left alliance, comprising diverse subordinated groups. The ideas elaborated here are intended to be of interest across that spectrum, not in a utopian merging, but in a pragmatic and purposeful sharing of strategic analyses and intuitions. My invoking of lesbian texts and theories should be understood in that light. I have written inclusively of lesbians and gay men wherever that has seemed plausible—but this signals a proposed political alignment, not an assertion that "we" are "the same" (indeed, not all gay men are the same). The twin dangers here are presuming to speak for others, and arrogantly excluding them. Writing "queer" doesn't resolve these problems, and I have used it in my title only after considerable hesitation. On the one hand, it may be too limiting—yielding up too easily the aspiration to hold a politics of class, race, and ethnicity alongside a politics of gender and sexuality. On the other, it may be over-ambitious. In Britain especially, many people outside activist circles still find "queer" too distressing for reappropriation; and there is still the danger that inclusion will lead to effacement. "Queer's inclusive, universalizing move vis-à-vis fellow-traveling outsiders tends to, once again, ensure that lesbian sexuality will remain *locked out of the visible*," Kate Davy says.[6] This danger is not evaded altogether by the present study, which has more to say about male homosexuality. Nevertheless, I have depended upon lesbian writers, and other subcultural groups also, and aspire to a broad political relevance.

This book derives from an invitation to give the Thomas Sovereign Gates, Jr. Lectures at the University of Pennsylvania in 1993. That occasion provoked an attempt to distill my sense of what is involved in a cultural materialist practice, while developing new work that would engage a distinguished audience. I have not felt constrained to publish the lectures as they were delivered. That period in Philadelphia involved all kinds of stimulating interactions with friends and colleagues, and it seems more substantially faithful to the occasion to offer in print the outcome of reflection upon all that. I am especially grateful to Dan Traister, Michael Ryan, Peter Stallybrass, Ann Rosalind Jones, Margreta de Grazia, Phyllis Rackin, Lynda Hart, Maureen Quilligan, Jerry Singerman, and Joseph X. Goins. I have also benefited crucially from the advice of Henry Abelove, Joseph Bristow, Richard Dellamora, Jonathan Dollimore, Thom Gunn, Gowan Hewlett, Laurence Lerner, Helena Reckitt, Simon Shepherd, and Talia Rodgers. My other inspiration has been students on the University of Sussex M.A. programme, Sexual Dissidence and Cultural Change. They have helped me to see what can be done.

1. Shakespeare and Dissident Reading

Flying Visit

Last time I traveled to the United States, before I could reach the airline desk in London, I met with the additional checks that have been provoked by fears of terrorism. Who was I? Why was I traveling? To the young security guard, I evidently didn't look like his idea of a professor. Anyway, professor of what? This was where the trouble really started. English Literature—he'd really hated that subject, he'd flunked out in that, he just couldn't stand English Literature.

Disaster: this man could detain me till it was too late to catch my flight. Another problem was that he couldn't work out why I might be going to talk about English, when they have lots of people there doing it already. Well, he was quite cute, and of course I was charming, so we joshed around a bit; eventually we were getting to be buddies. So he said: "OK, I'll test you. Who was the guy who wanted his pound of flesh?" "Got it!," I exclaimed: "Shylock in *The Merchant of Venice*." And, exhilarated that I was on the point of winning through, I added: "Isn't that a horrible play?" "YES!" he shouted, astonished at the convergence in our judgments, "Isn't that a horrible play!"

The young man was Jewish, I deduced. And my journey had been threatened by the insults he had experienced as a student, and by his belief that I must be committed to the universal wisdom and truth of *The Merchant*. "We don't do it like that any more," I told him: "now we talk about how Shakespeare got to write it that way, and why we don't like it. Cultural politics." "Is that what you do now?" he enthused, "That's what you do? That's just great!" So I gained an endorsement for at least some humanities work, and caught my plane.

There are various thoughts to ponder in this story. One group concerns the relationship between Englit in the U.K. and the United States; that underlies a good deal of this book. Another group of thoughts, of course, is about the still-dominant way of considering literary texts—as if they transcend political questions. For instance: in the midst of a shocking survey of anti-Semitic uses of *The Merchant*—from the eighteenth century to the present, from Nazi people to nice people such as Muriel Bradbrook and C.S. Lewis—John Gross proclaims: "Shylock would not have held the stage for four hundred years if he were a mere stereotype. His greatness is to be himself, to transcend the roles of representative Jew and conventional usurer." Louis Simpson, reviewing Gross's book in the *New York Times Book Review*, agrees: the play is "protean," "unexhausted," an "apparently timeless subject."[1]

For Philip Roth, in his novel *Operation Shylock*, it is the other way round. The powerful imaginative realization that Shakespeare has achieved is the problem:

> To the audiences of the world Shylock is the embodiment of the Jew in the way Uncle Sam embodies for them the spirit of the United States. Only, in Shylock's case, there is an overwhelming Shakespearean reality, a terrifying aliveness that your pasteboard Uncle Sam cannot begin to possess. . . . only the greatest English writer of them all could have had the prescience to isolate and dramatize as he did. You remember Shylock's opening line? You remember the three words? What Jew can forget them? What Christian can forgive them? *"Three thousand ducats."* Five blunt, unbeautiful English syllables and the stage Jew is elevated to its apogee by a genius, catapulted into eternal notoriety.[2]

It is not a question of accusing Shakespeare of "being racist"; he lived a long time ago when people thought differently about all kinds of things, and doubtless did his best to make sense of it, like most of us. And, as Gross observes, the Jewish stereotype does not derive from him. But, Gross admits, "he endowed it with his fame and prestige, and in a sense his humanising it only made it seem more plausible" (p. 287). It is a question of what the play tends to do, and may be made to do, in our cultures.

Of course, it might be objected that my security guard wasn't very well educated; that he wasn't reading "properly"—i.e., in the manner of Englit. Perhaps he had not been told, as Lillian S. Robinson was, to set aside anti-Semitism and address "the real point of the work." He had not been persuaded, as Lionel Trilling was, to embrace the reduction of "cultural diversity to what appeared, from an intellectual standpoint, to be the highest common denominator, the English cultural tradition." Trilling is famous partly as the first Jewish person to be hired to teach English at Columbia University; he is not known to have complained that *The Mer-*

chant was pressed upon him in high school.[3] The guard had not been trained to identify with the Christians against the Jews, as Adrienne Rich was. She recalls being given the role of Portia, despite being perceived as the only Jewish girl in the class, and urged (by her self-oppressed father) to say "the word 'Jew'" with "more scorn and contempt." She was encouraged "to pretend to be a non-Jewish child acting a non-Jewish character"—for "who would not dissociate from Shylock in order to identify with Portia?"[4]

If we accept any responsibility for the way our prized texts circulate beyond the academy, the routine classroom humiliation of ordinary readers from subordinated groups is our concern. That is why Shakespeare is political.

The reason for additional airport checks is that some people from other parts of the world feel so hijacked by the imperial pretensions of "western values" that they are prepared to blow us up. I can't even be sure the security guard was Jewish. He may have been an Arab annoyed at the representation of the Prince of Morocco, a feminist sympathizer objecting to the lively Portia marrying the unpleasant Bassanio, or a gay man affronted at the casual handling of Antonio's love for Bassanio. Observe the weakness of his position, though. He was protecting the physical security of "western values" and hence of the system that promotes *The Merchant*— as enshrined in the customary deference toward Shakespeare and largely reinforced by professional Englit. Yet, at the same time, there is cultural dissidence: there are radical readings, and a security guard can repudiate a part of Shakespeare. That is the field over which this book will be working.

Cultural Production

The ostensible project of literary criticism has been to seek the right answer to disputed readings, but in fact, we all know, the essay that purports to settle such questions always provokes another. This is because both literary writing and Englit are involved in the processes through which our cultures elaborate themselves. Three further things follow from this involvement; three central tenets of cultural materialism (which I discuss further in the next chapter).

First, the texts we call "literary" characteristically address contested aspects of our ideological formation. When a part of our worldview threatens disruption by manifestly failing to cohere with the rest, then we reorganize and retell its story, trying to get it into shape—back into the old shape if we are conservative-minded, or into a new shape if we are more adventurous. These I call "faultline" stories. They address the awkward, unresolved issues; they require most assiduous and continuous reworking; they hinge upon a fundamental, unresolved ideological complication that finds its way, willy-nilly, into texts. Through diverse literary genres and institutions, people write about faultlines, in order to address aspects of their life that they find hard to handle. There is nothing mysterious about this. Authors and readers want writing to be interesting, and these unresolved issues are the most promising for that.

Second, literature is only one of innumerable places where this production of culture occurs, but it is a relatively authoritative one, and Shakespeare is a powerful cultural token. He is already where meaning is produced, and people therefore want to get him on their side—to hijack him, we might say—as they do Madonna or the pope. Finding that Ben Jonson's *Sejanus* is against tyranny is worthwhile, but not likely to move people strongly. Consequently, publishers like books with Shakespeare in the title, examiners set him, the National Endowment for the Arts funds him. . . . It is only the person without cultural power—the security guard—who believes the repudiation (rather than the appropriation) of Shakespeare to be his best move.

Third, and consequently, there is no disinterested reading. Of course, we all know this, though it has been the historic project of Englit to efface it. But how could it be otherwise? The "universal" Shakespeare usually means the one we want to recruit as ratification for our point of view; with stunning presumption, we suppose that we have discovered the true version, whereas earlier generations were merely partial. Actually, Shakespearean texts, like other texts, are embedded in the histories from which they derive. Indeed, it is because of this that we can appropriate them so conveniently—it is the mismatch with present-day assumptions that allows us to make what we will of them. There is a continuity of sorts, to be sure; the wish to victimize outgroups, for instance, is found in many cultures. But that is not sufficiently specific. Of course *The Merchant of Venice* doesn't anticipate the Holocaust, or, indeed, Nazi persecution of homosexuals, but we may find it hard to approach the text without such an issue coming to mind. The inventiveness of directors and the subtleties of critics are designed, precisely, to bridge the historical gap. Shakespeare keeps going because these strategies keep him going; he is relevant because he is perpetually interfered with. Somewhat strangely, it is supposed that it would be better for literature if it were otherwise—if writers such as Shakespeare manifested a static and unchanging truth. But literary writing is interesting when it is in the thick of cultural production, along with movies, soaps, anthropology, religion, science fiction.

In India, Saguna Ramanathan explains, Jane Austen's *Persuasion* reads differently. Anne Eliot, allowing herself to be persuaded by Lady Russell not to marry the man she loves, "strikes the average Indian student as moral and correct; Indian society leads her to believe that her elders are to be respected and obeyed; they can, and must, determine her marriage choice." Again, Ania Loomba remarks, John Webster's *Duchess of Malfi* has specific resonances in India, where intra-familial violence may provoke recognition of a comparable oppression of widows today.[5]

Those should not be regarded as eccentric instances—there are more students reading English in the University of Delhi than in England. They point to just the kind of cultural contest in which literary writing has always been involved. For hundreds of years, whether you should marry someone you love or someone your parents approve was unresolved in western European and North American culture. It was held that the people marrying should act in obedience to their parents, so as to secure property relations—and also that they should love each other. Dutiful children experienced "an impossible conflict of role models," Lawrence Stone says. "They had to try to reconcile the often incompatible demands for obedience to parental wishes on the one hand and expectations of affection in marriage on the other."[6] At this point, patriarchy had not quite got its act together. The "divided duty," between father and husband, was not peculiarly Desdemona's problem, therefore, or Cordelia's; it is how the world was set up for women in that society. This faultline was explored in literary writing through the ensuing centuries. By the time of Jane Austen, most of the sentiment is on the side of the young lovers—though still it is better if the match turns out to be socially appropriate as well. The question dies out in fiction in the late nineteenth century because, for almost everyone, it is resolved in favor of children's preferences, and therefore no longer interesting. For North American or British Asians, however, it may well be a live question today—and hence appears in the film *Mississippi Masala* (1991), and in Hanif Kureishi's novel and television serial *The Buddha of Suburbia* (1991, 1993).

The Merchant, too, is a place where we have been working out our cultures. Since Henry Irving's stage interpretation of 1879, Shylock has often been presented more "sympathetically"—as provoked by Venetian hostility, perhaps achieving "tragic" stature. This approach is encapsulated in Helen Vendler's remark, which Christopher Ricks (in the course of a discussion of T.S. Eliot's anti-Semitism) has endorsed: "Shylock, in Shakespeare's imagination, grows in interest and stature so greatly that he incriminates the anti-Semitism of Belmont."[7] In a paradoxical sense, therefore, Shylock wins—not in the world, of course, but "in Shakespeare's imagination." In practice, I believe, such readings can be achieved only by leaning, tendentiously, on the text. Until Irving's 1879 production, Shylock had been presented as a monster; Irving's innovation was regarded with scepticism by such literary figures as Lord Houghton, James Spedding, John Ruskin, Henry James, George Bernard Shaw, William Poel, F.S. Boas, Sir Arthur Quiller-Couch, Frank Harris, and Elmer Edgar Stoll.[8] It is the same today. "I am against rewriting Shakespeare," declares David Thacker, director of the 1993 Royal Shakespeare Company production, "but I have only been able to direct *The Merchant of Venice* by shifting its perspective."[9]

Yet even a "sympathetic" presentation, with Shylock as victim, is not good enough. However cunningly slanted, it can hardly avoid some version of the proposition that the Christians are as bad as the Jews—who function, thereby, as an index of badness. Typically, this notion will be accompanied by an assertion that we possess a common humanity (or inhumanity—it comes to the same thing), but still there is an underlying us-and-them pattern. The liberal reading of Joseph Conrad's *Heart of Darkness* works in this way: we (i.e., we Europeans) are as bad as, or even worse than, the savages over there. The Jewish playwright Arnold Wesker objects that "sympathetic" versions of *The Merchant* are patronizing and, anyway, don't actually work. However the play is handled in the theater, "the image comes through inescapably: the Jew is mercenary and revengeful, sadistic, without pity." And "the so-called defence of Shylock," Wesker says, with Laurence Olivier's National Theatre production of 1973 in mind, "was so powerful that it dignified the anti-semitism. An audience, it seemed to me on that night, could come away with its prejudices about the Jew confirmed but held with an easy conscience because they thought they'd heard a noble plea for extenuating circumstances."[10] In *Shylock*, Wesker's rewrite, the normally kindly Jew is angry at just one point: when Lorenzo embarks complacently on the topic, "After all, has not a Jew eyes?" Shylock says: "I do not want apologies for my humanity. Plead for me no special pleas. I will not have my humanity mocked and apologized for. If I am unexceptionally like any man then I need no exceptional portraiture. I merit no special pleas, no special cautions, no special gratitudes. My humanity is my right, not your bestowed and gracious privilege" (p. 255). The speech that humanists generally celebrate as redeeming Shakespeare's play is, by virtue of such a program of redemption, perceived as condescending.

Wesker contests *The Merchant* by rewriting it. Terry Eagleton offers a subversive critical re-reading. Shylock is not the victim, Eagleton declares, but the victor: he "is triumphantly vindicated even though he loses the case: he has forced the Christians into outdoing his own 'inhuman' legalism"; he unmasks "Christian justice as a mockery."[11] In this version, Shylock's vindication is not accomplished through his suffering, and does not depend upon a vague notion of imaginative stature. There is a specific contradiction, one that exposes the power-structure of Venice: it is Shylock who has respect for the spirit of the law, Portia who resorts to hyper-ingenious quibbling. Further, Eagleton finds virtue in contracts, rather than in Christian charity or mercy. It is "the victimized that need a fixed contract, however hard-hearted that may seem, precisely because they would be foolish to rely on the generosity of their oppressors." Gratuitous mercy is all very well, but "the dispossessed can never quite know when their superiors are likely to be seized with a spontaneous bout of geniality" (p. 41). However, Eagleton's brilliant readings depend on starting out with a purposeful scepticism about authority—as with his claim that the Witches are "the heroines" of *Macbeth*. "To any unprejudiced reader—which would seem to exclude Shakespeare himself, his contemporary audiences and almost all literary critics—it is surely clear that positive value in *Macbeth* lies with the three witches" (pp. 1–2). Eagleton is reading, cheekily, perhaps destructively, against the grain—showing both how the text may be made to disclose a dissident perspective, and how much forcing that may require.

"Sympathetic" presentations of Shylock have been contested also by right-wingers. Allan Bloom says Shylock asks for trouble by having "the soul of a man who has refused to assimilate. He is consequently distrusted and hated. He reciprocates, and his soul is poisoned."[12] So it serves Shylock right, for not abandoning his own culture and adopting "western values." In his book *The Closing of the American Mind*, Bloom aims to assert the importance and enduring truth of the traditional humanities. His reading of *The Merchant* exposes the coercion in such a project—the extent to which it entails the systematic subordination of subcultures. Portia and the Venetians are right to punish Shylock, Bloom says: "Venice is a Christian city, and Antonio her husband's friend. If the cancer of civil discord must be rooted out, then Shylock is the one to go."[13] However, western values are not so conveniently at Bloom's bidding as he wants us to infer: he too leans on the text to strengthen his position in the cultural contest. He evaluates Portia's unsuccessful suitors—the princes of Morocco and Arragon—on racial principles supposedly deriving from their geographical locations: "The South [Morocco] is barbaric; the North [Arragon], cold and sententious. True civilization [Venice] implies a mixture of developed understanding and reflection with a full capacity to perceive" (p. 26). Now, if you look at a map of Europe, Arragon is to the south of Venice; so if its prince represents the inadequacies of the north, Portia's Venetian suitor, Bassanio, must display an Arctic iciness, rather than the ideal balance attributed to him by Bloom. Shakespeare could easily have specified a markedly northern prince; *The Merchant* does not confirm Bloom's ideological geography. The moral he wants to draw is clear enough: to be an acceptable person you must not be foreign, or maintain any adherence to an ethnic culture. Otherwise you deserve what you get. Actually, history shows that when they want a scapegoat conforming won't protect you.

Shakespeare and Sex

Here is another minority reading: of Shakespeare's poem *Venus and Adonis*. The goddess Venus is trying to seduce Adonis, a beautiful but rather petulant young man. He is reluctant:

> He sees her coming, and begins to glow,
> Even as a dying coal revives with wind;
> And with his bonnet hides his angry brow,
> Looks on the dull earth with disturbed mind,
>   Taking no notice that she is so nigh,
>   For all askance he holds her in his eye.[14]

John Addington Symonds, the Victorian man of letters, read this before he was ten, and it changed his life. Hitherto, what Symonds calls his "reveries" had generally "reverted" to "naked sailors." But then he read Shakespeare's poem:

> It gave form, ideality and beauty to my previous erotic visions. Those adult males, the shaggy and brawny sailors, without entirely disappearing, began to be superseded in my fancy by an adolescent Adonis. The emotion they sym-

bolized blent with a new kind of feeling. In some confused way I identified myself with Adonis; but at the same time I yearned after him as an adorable object of passionate love. Venus only served to intensify the situation. I did not pity her. I did not want her. I did not think that, had I been in the position of Adonis, I should have used his opportunities to better purpose. No: she only expressed my own relation to the desirable male. . . . I dreamed of falling back like her upon the grass, and folding the quick-panting lad in my embrace.[15]

Suppose, Symonds wonders, his predisposition had been heterosexual? "Boys of more normal sexuality might have preferred the 'Rape of Lucrece'," he says (rather a chilling thought). Or, in *Venus and Adonis*, "they might have responded to the attraction of the female—condemning Adonis for a simpleton, and wishing themselves for ten minutes in his place" (p. 63). People from minorities read differently; and women, surely, might want to make of the poem something different again.

I am moving between gay and Jewish subordinations here, with a glance toward South Asian women, because I don't want these arguments tidied away as the preoccupation, the special pleading of any one minority; by the end of this book, I mean to undermine the central project of mainstream Englit. In fact, as has often been pointed out, there are two outsiders in *The Merchant*. Antonio is a merchant who courts an aristocratic set by lending them money without interest; he is in love with Bassanio and, striving to appease the dominant group, despises another outgroup, Jews. Like Shylock, he is acceptable while he provides finance, but he is not at home at Belmont; if he became as assertive as Shylock, no doubt he would get comparably brisk treatment.[16]

Symonds believed that he had taken *Venus and Adonis* "in the way Shakespeare undoubtedly meant it to be taken." That is how cultural hijacking works—everyone claims to have the true reading. Yet suddenly the question is topical: can Shakespeare be claimed as gay? In 1992 I was asked to write about it for a national newspaper, and to speak about it for a television series called *Dark Horses* (the other featured artists were Michelangelo and D.H. Lawrence). The issue was stimulated in Britain by director Tim Luscombe's idea that his London Gay Theatre Company might perform Shakespeare with a distinctive slant—playing up "the gay relationship between Horatio and Hamlet," for instance. This stirred the U.K. tabloid newspapers into fervent mockery. Likely titles were offered—*The Fairy Wives of Windsor, Tight-Ass Andronicus*.

Like literature and art, theater is widely regarded as an effeminate practice. But Shakespeare at least has seemed reassuringly manly, with big tragic and historical themes, robust comedy, plenty of fighting, "bawdy" (i.e., sexist) language. Marriage to a proper man seems to be the answer to most problems, unless he is Black. In the history plays, manliness correlates with Englishness—hence the customary critical pleasure in Prince Hal's mis-spent youth and Henry V's rough-and-ready domination of his French fiancée. Those not at Agincourt will "hold their manhoods cheap," the king says. Wimps such as Richard II and Henry VI fail to rule us with the strong hand that we need—the latter is called "an effeminate prince."

Of course, queer nuances have been an easy move in Shakespeare productions since John Barton's 1969 *Troilus and Cressida*. It is the obvious thing to do with the two characters called Antonio, in *Twelfth Night* and *The Merchant*. But the price for this has been that these characters appear squalid, frivolous, or sad. This is not the only, or even the most reasonable interpretation of them. There is no scholarly-historical reason why the Antonio characters should not continue in close relationships with their boy-friends, whose marriages are evidently more opportunist than passionate. It is our cultures that imagine that when heterosexual relations occur alongside homosexual relations, the straight relation must win out—as if a biological destiny were asserting itself.

Yet there has been a persistent undercurrent of anxiety. Well before our self-conscious times, others noticed something of what Symonds found in *Venus and Adonis*. Max Wolff, in 1907, was disconcerted that "the beauty of the youth" was represented as enthusiastically as that of Venus, and ascribed it to Shakespeare being "a true son of the Renaissance, bred in Platonic ideas." "We," he says—we heterosexuals, he means—"we take a different, doubtless less liberal point of view than did the sixteenth century. We do not share in sensuous admiration of the male figure. Especially when it comes from the lips of a woman it oversteps the bounds of our conception of propriety and offends us by the frankness of its physical desire."[17] Douglas Bush in 1932 found *Venus and Adonis* distastefully unmasculine. Shakespeare "fiddles on the strings of sensuality without feeling or awakening . . . sympathy, without even being robustly sensual"; he is "content with prettiness, and the poem, though far from languid, is sicklied o'er with effeminacy." Interestingly, Bush prefers Christopher Marlowe's *Hero and Leander*, which he finds "strong, masculine, swift."[18]

Then there is cross-dressing in the comedies. Until recently, criticism closed this down, saying it was merely conventional and made no difference, and harping on the eventual marriages. But with boys playing girls who are playing boys making love to girls, who are actually boys, even the most conventional critic might wonder whether something strange is going on. In a celebrated study, *Shakespeare's Festive Comedy* (1959), C.L. Barber celebrates the marriages at the end of *Twelfth Night*, declaring that readers and audiences will appreciate them as "wish-fulfilment"; he is pleased that "playful reversal of sexual roles can renew the meaning of the normal relation."[19] However, Barber is obliged to register an awkwardness in the bizarre way a boy character is substituted for a girl. His response is that he will put up with anything so long as manliness triumphs: "The particular implausibility that there should be an identical man to take Viola's place with Olivia is submerged in the general, beneficent realization," he says, "that there is such a thing as a man" (p. 246).

Coppélia Kahn, in her book *Man's Estate*, similarly endorses the eventual straightening out of these characters: "*Twelfth Night* traces the evolution of sexuality as related to identity, from the playful and unconscious toyings of youthful courtship, through a period of sexual confusion, to a final thriving in which swagger is left behind and men and women truly know themselves through choosing and loving the right mate."[20] You "know yourself" when you become heterosexual. Lately, the topic of cross dressing in the comedies has been reopened, to exciting effect.[21]

Shakespeare's sonnets have caused most anxiety. Arthur Hallam's father, nervous about the intense relationship between his son and the poet Alfred Tennyson, complained: "it is impossible not to wish that Shakespeare had never written them. There is a weakness and folly in all excessive and mis-placed affection, which is not redeemed by the touches of nobler sentiments."[22] Tennyson, of course, is another suspect figure. On the four U.K. postage stamps commemorating the centenary of his death in 1992, four of his exotic feminine creations are pictured emerging from his manly bardic brow, but there is no sign of the young male friend who inspired his best poetry.

Quite a lot may be sacrificed in order to dispel the specter of bardic queerness. Eric Partridge, in his study *Shakespeare's Bawdy* (1947), supported the idea that "most of the Sonnets may be read as literary exercises." It seemed safer to abandon the integrity of the poetry than to admit that Shakespeare might have been like that. Not that the bard was a bigot, of course. According to Partridge, his attitude to homosexuality is evident in "much the same sort of kindly-contemptuous or unmawkish-pitying remark as the averagely tolerant and understanding person of the present generation would make" (even in your kindness you will of course be contemptuous, even in your pity you must be careful not to be mawkish).[23] Shakespeare, I have observed, is a powerful cultural token, a figure to get on your side; Partridge doesn't want him hijacked for homosexuality. Nevertheless, he quotes a "medical man" saying that "none of us can pride ourselves on being a hundred per cent. man or a hundred per cent. woman" (p.14), thereby managing to leave the hint of androgyny that produces Shakespeare as the ultimate artist and human being.

The Earl of Southampton has long been proposed as the beautiful young man for whom Shakespeare may have written the Sonnets and *Venus and Adonis*. A recent biographer of Shakespeare, Garry O'Connor, contains the danger by pigeonholing Southampton, Shakespeare, and Marlowe in modern stereotypes. The earl had an "intensely feminised" nature, O'Connor says, and "played up to his admirers . . . with a dark and neurotic mixture of arrogance and bashfulness" (treacherous queer). Marlowe, who had a "dark taste," fell for it: he conceived a "passion for Southampton"—though it was "pure wish-fulfilment" on Marlowe's part (silly queen).[24] But Shakespeare, O'Connor asserts, was interested only in Southampton's patronage; he was "far too mindful of his own skin to write sonnets of homosexual love" (p. 143). Again, integrity is a price worth paying to secure heterosexuality. Notice, though, how conceding Marlowe permits Shakespeare to shine through as the one complete man/supreme artist.

Exeunt *Jupiter* cum *Ganymede*

Shakespeare can't have been gay; not because the bard could not have been so disreputable, but because in his time they didn't have the concept. Recent historical work on homosexuality has mostly started from Michel Foucault's thesis in *The History of Sexuality: An Introduction*: early-modern England did not have a concept of "the homosexual." The big shift occurs in the nineteenth century, when the person who engages in same-sex activity (the term is designed to avoid anachronism) gets to be perceived as a type of person. So far from the Victorians repressing sex, Foucault brilliantly observes, they went on about it all the time; it became a principal mode of social regulation. As part of this process, the "homosexual became a personage, a past, a case history, and a childhood, in addition to being a type of life, a life form, and a morphology, with an indiscreet anatomy and possibly a mysterious physiology. . . . The sodomite had been a temporary aberration; the homosexual was now a species."[25] The difference is between taking things from a chain-store, which many young-sters might do at some time, and being labeled "a thief": with the latter, thievishness is made to seem the core of your personality.

Alan Bray, in his book *Homosexuality in Renaissance England*, substan-tiates much of Foucault's case. In Shakespeare's time, Bray shows, the usual legal and medical terms for same-sex practices were sodomy and buggery, but these were (by our notions) ill-defined, and they were not specialized as the kind of thing only a certain kind of person might do. They were framed within "a more general notion: debauchery; and debauchery was a temptation to which all, in principle at least, were subject." The sodomist was not distinctively effeminate—transvestism was not a sign of same-sex passion, but "a vice in its own right."[26]

As commentators have pointed out, there are several snags in this argument. First, paintings and fictive texts sometimes indicate a more positive attitude toward same-sex passion than the legal and ethical sources Bray mainly used. He believed it would have been virtually impossible to self-identify as a sodomite, so disreputable was that idea, and he set aside fictive evidence. However, as I have argued, we should regard "literary" writing as a prestigious formation through which faultline stories circulate. As Bray now agrees, fictive writing has to be plausible, however obliquely; it must indicate something about the place of same-sex practices in the culture that promoted it. Bruce Smith proposes in *Homosexual Desire in Shake-speare's England* that we should recognize different kinds of discourse: moral, legal, medical, and poetic. Same-sex practices were valued dis-tinctively in poetic writing, largely contradicting moral and legal discourses, because of the huge prestige of ancient Greek and Roman texts. The intellectual and rhetorical sophistication of classical writings was hard to equal, and they planted in the midst of a mainly Christian culture powerful images of forbidden sexualities (it was the same with respect to religion).[27] Smith discovers, not a homosexual identity in the modern sense, but six "cultural scenarios" for same-sex relations, founded in classical sources: heroic friendship, men and boys (mainly in pastoral and educational con-texts), playful androgyny (mainly in romances and festivals), transvestism (mainly in satirical contexts), master-servant relations, and an emergent homosexual subjectivity (in Shakespeare's sonnets). Within such a network of possibilities, individuals might negotiate quite diverse sexual alignments.

A second, underlying problem is the Foucauldian principle that his-tory falls into epochs, characterized by distinct modes of thought, with change occurring through a sequence of large-scale epistemological shifts. This position makes his theories vulnerable to any scrap of empirical evidence showing ideas or behaviors occurring at the "wrong" time. However, it is a mistake to expect an even development, whereby one model characterizes an epoch and then is superseded by another. There may have been in early-modern Europe, especially in highly privileged circles, coteries where something like our concept of the homosexual individual occurred. That concept need not have been generally known, and need not have been coherent with, or even have affected, wider patterns of sexuality and gender. Ideology is never tidy, though ideologues present it as though it were. So, even if certain figures were recognizably continuous with our idea of "a homosexual," a gay identity might still be inaccessible—incomprehensible—to almost everyone.

I have a suspicion that the quest for the moment at which the modern homosexual subject is constituted is misguided. I suspect that what we call gay identity has, for a long time, been always in the process of getting constituted—as the middle classes have been always rising, or, more pertinently, as the modern bourgeois subject has for a long time been in the process of getting constituted. Theorists of post-structuralism—Catherine Belsey, Francis Barker, Jonathan Dollimore, Joel Fineman, Jonathan Goldberg, Simon Shepherd—sometimes write as if they were showing that Shakespeare and his contemporaries did not envisage full or even coherent subjectivities in anything like the modern way.[28] But actually these scholars tend to discover ambivalent or partial signs of subjectivity; they catch not the absence of the modern subject, but its emergence. It may be that such analyses reveal, not a moment of decisive change, but a continuing process. Of course, the human subject is never full, and hence may, at any moment, appear unformed. And so with gay subjectivity, which because of its precarious social position is anyway more fragile and inconstant: it is on-going, we are still discovering it. For the development of gay subjects must, of course, be dependent on the development of subjects at large. The further, enticing thought is that it may also be the other way around: that the development of the modern subject is in some ways dependent on the development of the gay subject.

The crucial point running through these explorations is that early-modern Britons drew the boundaries of sexualities in different places from those where we draw them. In particular, they did not associate male same-sex practices specifically with "effeminacy." This is a key part of the modern construct of the homosexual. It involves, as Foucault puts it, "a certain way

of inverting the masculine and the feminine in oneself. Hom
appeared as one of the forms of sexuality when it was transpos(
practice of sodomy onto a kind of interior androgyny, a hermap....
of the soul."[29] This is the dominant modern notion: it lurks behind the
female soul in the male body (the doctrine of sexologists at the turn of the
century); it informs, in Freud, the Oedipal failure to identify with the
"right" parent; and it appears, still today, in radical ideas about the transgressive impact of gender-bending.

A lot of people want to talk about "masculinity" at the moment, but
"effeminacy" remains too awkward to address. My quotation marks indicate that there is nothing essential about either—that they are ideological
constructs. Effeminacy is founded in misogyny: the root idea is of a male
falling away from the purposeful reasonableness that is supposed to constitute manliness, into the laxity and weakness conventionally attributed
to women. The connotations in the *Oxford English Dictionary* are:
"womanish, unmanly, enervated, feeble; self-indulgent, voluptuous; unbe-
comingly delicate or over-refined." Effeminacy is a way of stigmatizing
deviation from orthodox gender stereotypes. The effeminate male is (1)
"wrong" and (2) inferior (female); the "masculine" woman, conversely, is
(1) "wrong" and (2) impertinent (aspiring to manliness). The former may
be despised, the latter resented for her presumption. The effect is a policing of sexual categories, and it extends vastly beyond lesbians and gay men.
The whole order of sexuality and gender is pinioned by the fears and
excitements that gather around the allegedly inappropriate distribution of
gender categories.

Until the Oscar Wilde trials in 1895, I think—far later than is generally
supposed—it is unsafe to interpret effeminacy as defining of, or as a signal
of, same-sex passion.[30] Mostly, it meant being emotional and spending too
much time with women. Thus it often involved excessive cross-sexual
attachment. To be manly was of course to go with women, but in a way
that did not forfeit mastery. Basically, effeminacy and same-sex passion did
not correlate in the way that is commonly expected today. In Milton's
Samson Agonistes, Samson's explanation of his subjection to Dalila is that
"foul effeminacy held me yoked / Her bondslave."[31] Shakespeare's Romeo
says he is effeminate—not in respect of his love for Mercutio, but when he
is distressed at his failure to prevent the death of Mercutio. Juliet's beauty
"hath made me effeminate," he says. It is love for a woman that produces
the problem for masculinity; had Romeo been swayed more strongly by
his love for Mercutio, that would have been manly.[32]

One model of same-sex passion involved the lord and his minion—the catamite, the Ganymede. In Shakespeare's *Troilus and Cressida*, Thersites calls Patroclus "boy" and accuses him of being Achilles's "Male varlet," "his masculine whore." There is an imputation of effeminacy; Patroclus has "little stomach to the war" (line 219). However, it does not attach to Achilles—not with respect to his relationship with Patroclus. Achilles is warned about effeminacy because of his devotion to a woman, Hector's sister Polyxena:

> A woman impudent and mannish grown
> Is not more loath'd than an effeminate man
> In time of action.[33]

That is Patroclus speaking; "Sweet, rouse yourself," he says to Achilles (line 221). But the relationship between Achilles and Patroclus is not the problem, because it does not compete with warrior values. As Bruce Smith observes, satirists applied the insulting term "Ganymede," "not to sodomites in general, but only to the younger, passive partner who serves another man's pleasure." A real man was entitled to indulge himself as and where he would; only the inferior partner was despised. "Female," Smith shows, was "but one way among many of signifying one male's subjection to another."[34] This was the key distinction in ancient Greece, David Halperin points out: "the relation between the 'active' and the 'passive' sexual partner is thought of as the same kind of relation as that obtaining between social superior and social inferior." Anyone who is not a man, defined as taking the "active" role in sexual practice, must be some kind of woman. Recent studies have shown similar assumptions today in Turkey, Thailand, and Latin America.[35]

Marlowe's *Dido Queen of Carthage* begins with Jupiter playing with Ganymede. Venus complains:

> Ay, this is it: you can sit toying there,
> And playing with that female wanton boy,
> Whiles my Aeneas wanders on the sea
> And rests a prey to every billow's pride.[36]

Jupiter is blamed for playing with a "female wanton boy" when there is imperial business to be done; Ganymede is "female" because Jupiter is playing with him. Jupiter agrees to sort out Aeneas's mission and exits—with Ganymede: "*Exeunt* Jupiter *cum* Ganymede." The problem is the imperial business, not the boy. Aeneas, too, is effeminate when he neglects his imperial destiny, but this time the distraction is a woman. His comrade Achates exhorts:

> Banish that ticing dame from forth your mouth,
> And follow your foreseeing stars in all;
> This is no life for men-at-arms to live,
> Where dalliance doth consume a soldier's strength,
> And wanton motions of alluring eyes
> Effeminate our minds inur'd to war. (IV.iii.31–36)

Unmanly behavior is attending to the feminine at the expense of heroic responsibility. This is the anxiety in *Antony and Cleopatra*. The Romans are dubious about Antony's devotion to Cleopatra, but while he is dominating an empire none of their suspicions really sticks. The cautious Octavius gets called "boy." Antony can dress up in Cleopatra's clothes and she can wear his sword, and there is no clear threat to his masculinity. A real man can do whatever he chooses; after all, Hercules, with whom Antony is identified, dressed up as a woman.[37] But it is an ambitious project, fit only for heroes. When Antony allows Cleopatra to determine the conduct of the war, and begins to lose, these feminizing practices seem to indicate his weakness and dependency.

More surprisingly to many people today, two warriors may proclaim mutual affection comparable to that between man and woman. So long as they are being very warrior-like, there is no embarrassment in carrying over the paradigm of cross-sexual relations. Coriolanus, in Shakespeare's play, compares his embrace of his comrade Cominius to his honeymoon night:

> Oh! let me clip ye
> In arms as sound as when I woo'd; in heart
> As merry as when our nuptial day was done,
> And tapers burn'd to bedward.[38]

This is not a psychological disturbance peculiar to Coriolanus; in warrior culture they all do it. "Flower of warriors," Cominius calls Coriolanus in response (line 32). Aufidius's greeting to Coriolanus is in the same vein:

> Know thou first,
> I lov'd the maid I married; never man
> Sigh'd truer breath; but that I see thee here,

> Thou noble thing, more dances my rapt heart
> Than when I first my wedded mistress saw
> Bestride my threshold. (IV.v.114–19)

Coriolanus usurps the place of the maid Aufidius married, but he does not become feminine. It is submitting to the Citizens that risks that:

> Away my disposition, and possess me
> Some harlot's spirit! My throat of war be turn'd,
> Which quired with my drum, into a pipe
> Small as a eunuch, or the virgin voice
> That babies lull asleep! (III.ii.111–5)

So does submitting to women—Coriolanus's wife and mother. Dependency makes him feminine—"at his nurse's tears / He whin'd and roar'd away your victory" (V.vi.97–98), Aufidius complains. And it reduces Coriolanus to that passive subordinate, a boy—which is what Thersites calls Patroclus, and Antony calls Octavius. "Thou boy of tears," Aufidius accuses (V.vi.101). The change that produces this taunt is not that Coriolanus has become a homosexual, but that he has submitted to women. This shifts his relations with men out of the heroic friendship model and into the Ganymede model.

Conclusion

Engaging in same-sex practices, then, didn't make you either a homosexual or effeminate; in certain circumstances it made you specially masculine. This warrior mode was entirely unlike the situation in our cultures today, where, as Eve Sedgwick has observed, the cement of male homosocial bonding is hostility toward homosexuality (repressed and/or overt). Early-modern culture had a different pattern; as Sedgwick says, "the structure of homosocial continuums [must be] culturally contingent, not an innate feature of either 'maleness' or 'femaleness'."[39] "So our virtues / Lie in th' interpretation of the time," Aufidius remarks (IV.vii.49–50).

Above all, perhaps, the situation was confused. In a 1991 article, "Male Friendship in Elizabethan England," Bray shows that the signals of male friendship—meaning the whole relation of kinship and patronage—overlapped with those of sodomy. He writes of "the unwelcome difficulty the Elizabethans had in drawing a dividing line between those gestures of closeness among men that they desired so much and those they feared."[40]

In similar vein, Jonathan Goldberg in his book *Sodometries* regards the very impossibility of sodomy not as closing down the topic, but as having afforded scope for innumerable deviant sexual acts in early-modern societies. Except when their perpetrators seemed to disturb the social order, these were rarely apprehended *as* sodomy—precisely because that was so unthinkable. Disavowal, in the very act of repudiating, invokes that which it hopes to banish. The goal of analysis, therefore, is not to track down gay writers or characters, but "to see what the category [sodomy] enabled and disenabled, and to negotiate the complex terrains, the mutual implications of prohibition and production."[41] The point is hardly who did what with whom, but what was perceived as being done, and the anxieties that informed such perceptions. Sodomy was a continual threat around the edges of male bonding. It is not a matter of whether Coriolanus and Aufidius fucked, but of the text being unable, and perhaps unwilling, to dispel the ghost of such an inference.

So the early-modern organization of sex and gender boundaries, simply, was different from ours. And therefore Shakespeare couldn't have been gay. However, that need not stem the panic, because, by the same token, he couldn't have been straight either. In practice, the plays are pervaded with erotic interactions that strike chords for lesbians and gay men today—as they did for Symonds. Friendships are conducted with a passion that would now be considered suspicious; language of sexual flirtation is used in circumstances where we would find it embarrassing; and all the female parts may, legitimately, be played by young men. It is not, necessarily, that Shakespeare was a sexual radical; rather, the ordinary currency of his theater and society is sexy for us. Shakespeare may work with distinct force for gay men and lesbians, simply because he didn't think he had to sort out sexuality in modern terms. For approximately the same reasons, these plays may incite radical ideas about gender, class, race, and nation.

So what is the status of Symonds's interpretation of *Venus and Adonis*, and of Jewish responses to *The Merchant*? Valerie Traub picks up a reading of *Twelfth Night* that assumes Olivia is punished "comically but unmistakably" for her same-sex passion for Viola. "To whom is desire between women funny?" Traub asks.[42] What is the status of a lesbian response? Shakespeare is said to speak to all sorts and conditions, but when a gay man or a Jew or a lesbian says "Yes, this is how he speaks to us"—that is disallowed. My point is not that reading as if one were someone else is necessarily a bad thing. It is salutary for most of us to imagine ourselves in another situation, especially when that involves intuiting a less powerful formation from a more powerful one, but it is not good for subordinated minorities to feel obliged to ventriloquize more powerful groups. William J. Bennett says, of "students": "If their past is hidden from them, they will become aliens in their own culture, strangers in their own land."[43] This is a true and moving sentiment, but applied in a manipulative way. For whose past is it, and which culture? Native American? Black? Vietnamese? By insisting upon the one superior, homogenizing, hegemonic "past," under the threat of stigmatization as "alien," Bennett pressures diverse peoples to repudiate their actual histories. The precise tendency of Englit, especially in its current, meritocratic phase, is to detach individuals from other subcultural allegiances. One abandons subculture to become Man.

In the rest of this book I attempt to develop a theory of culture and a critical practice that might respond to such awareness. In the next chapter, more historically and more abstractly, I try to explain what some of us have been trying to do under the banner of cultural materialism, and why. After that I focus upon an instance: the United States in the postwar period, with special reference to Tennessee Williams. Finally I address how and why Englit may be disrupted by readings sponsored out of lesbian and gay and other subcultural allegiances.

One further comment upon the Foucault-Bray thesis. It would be rash to suppose that now, in contradistinction to early-modern England, we all have a clear idea of male gay identity, and that gay men all live it; and that heterosexual men are altogether distinct from all that. This would be almost as violent a tidying-up of a complex and mobile field as the imposing of such identities on early-modern England. Goldberg points out that the first English sodomy statute, enacted in the time of Henry VIII, is cited verbatim, still, in the laws of six states of the USA and appears with small variations in others.[44] The topic remains immensely confused; and that is why, and how, it is still doing so much ideological work. So perhaps neither *Venus and Adonis*, nor Symonds's response to it, is as strange and remote as it may seem. Perhaps Symonds's reading is and was valid—not as the one, true reading, but as a haunting possibility that may be ignored or repudiated but will not go away.

2. Art as Cultural Production

Ideology

Students and professors in the United States often ask me to explain cultural materialism. This is mainly because it comes up in discussions of new historicism—either as a lamentable extreme toward which new historicism declines, or as the positive vision which it fails to attain. This is partly because the success of new historicism in North America derives from its vagueness; it covers most clever work that is not celebrating the unity of the-text-on-the-page. However, cultural materialism cannot adequately be understood as a variation on new historicism. It is a response, within British Marxism and Cultural Studies, to broader historical circumstances.

The European war of 1939–45 was unprecedented in the way it involved the whole population; it was called in Britain "the people's war." On the right as well as the left, it was agreed that there should be no return to the conditions of the 1930s. Then there had seemed to be three kinds of future: fascism, communism, and a rejigging of capitalism to protect people against exploitation and slumps—welfare-capitalism. These three fought it out between 1917 and 1948: fascism was defeated, and Europe was divided between communism and welfare-capitalism. Both promised all the people a stake in the society, an adequate share of its resources as of right—a job, a pension or social security, a roof over your head, health-care, education. In communism these were to be secured through state management of the economy; in welfare-capitalism, by state intervention in the capitalist economy in the manner proposed by John Maynard Keynes. In the United States, welfare-capitalism has often been imagined as socialism, but that is an index of the extent to which the Cold War wiped out the US left; actually welfare-capitalism is an attempt to ameliorate and preserve capitalism, by protecting against and compensating for its disadvantages.

It is popularly imagined that the west-European left has been crucially dismayed by the recent failure of the Soviet system. Actually, it is a long time since very many of us looked hopefully in that direction. Since the late 1950s, the west-European left has been preoccupied, whether its formal allegiance is constitutional or revolutionary, with the failure of our own system: welfare-capitalism. It seemed unable to produce either the general material wealth or the spirit of co-operative advance that had been antici-pated. The good life got to be defined as more household gadgets; and the idea that we had attained, or were about to attain, the best possible society was being used by politicians to make dissidence appear unnecessary and destructive. Despite the promises of 1945, we were suffering the ineffi-ciency and inhumanity of capitalism, of imperialism, of patriarchy.

By 1960 or so, therefore, it seemed evident that some further inter-vention of a socialist kind was still necessary. The first task was to define it in a way that did not run into the disadvantages we observed in the Soviet Bloc; that produced a nervousness about grappling with what was per-ceived as Marxism. The tougher problem was how to get an alternative program on the road. There were ample signs of social distress—crime and juvenile delinquency, strikes and bloody-mindedness, the dissolution of family and neighborhood bonds, drug abuse, racism. "Arise ye starv'lings from your slumbers," we cried. But for the most part they didn't—we didn't. We pondered the reasons, and deduced that people must have been got at. The revolution wasn't occurring because the continuing oppression of ordinary people was being obscured. It seemed, therefore, a failure *at the level of culture*. Hence the preoccupation, in the west-European left, with theories of ideology: that is what needs explaining.

The Frankfurt School blamed monopoly capitalism and the mass media: both high culture and traditional local cultures were being smoth-ered, and with them any sense of individual dignity. This was widely believed (I am aware that Frankfurt School work was not a postwar, west-European product; I am referring to the way it was taken up within that situation). More interestingly, Herbert Marcuse, in his essay "Repressive Tolerance" (1965), sought to explain the ineffectiveness of those who should have been dissident: liberals, who respected the utilitarian-bourgeois tradition. Though those values were still frequently invoked, Marcuse said, the structures of business, the military and the political system were over-riding them. He summed up: "The tolerance which is the great achieve-ment of the liberal era is still professed and (with strong qualifications) practiced, while the economic and political process is subjected to an ubiquitous and effective administration in accordance with the predomi-nant interests. The result is an objective contradiction between the economic and political structure on the one side, and the theory and practice of toleration on the other." Even the exercise of such freedoms as we appear to have—such as writing to your senator—strengthens repressive tendencies "by testifying to the existence of democratic liberties which, in reality, have changed their content and lost their effectiveness."[1] The very traditions and institutions that seemed to manifest the promise of freedom were inveigling people into complicity.

Marcuse's was a humanistic Marxism, founded in the belief that our humanity is there—it just needs liberating. Such a theory could flip over, quite easily, into revolutionary optimism. In the enthusiasm of the worldwide disturbances that we call "1968"—on U.S. campuses, in U.S. ghettoes, in Paris, Vietnam, Czechoslovakia, Cuba, and China; in the enthusiasm of all that, Marcuse was to make that optimistic move (in *An Essay on Liberation*, 1969). The appeal of Louis Althusser's essay "Ideology and Ideological State Apparatuses" (trans. 1971), coming in the wake of 1968, lay in its pessimism: Althusser at least could not raise extravagant hopes. "In order to exist," he declares, "every social formation must reproduce the conditions of its production."[2] This means both material resources and labour power. Immediately, this is done by wages, which enable workers to keep body and soul together so that they can check in at the workplace as required. But also, workers must accept their place in the system: there must be "a reproduction of submission to the ruling ideology for the workers, and a reproduction of the ability to manipulate the ruling ideology correctly for the agents of exploitation and repression" (pp. 127–28). People get socialized, in other words, into attitudes that facilitate maintenance of the system. Althusser's analysis here is very powerful indeed. By definition, societies that continue must be reproducing themselves ideologically as well as materially; they develop ideological apparatuses to arrange this—churches, schools, the family, the law, the political system, trades unions, the communications system, cultural arrangements. If they did not, they would die out or be transformed. Of course, there are directly repressive apparatuses as well—the police, courts, prisons, army. But in our societies—and to the west-European left this was the problem—people seem mostly to do what they are supposed to do. That compliance is what Althusser is addressing.

Further, this theory is not to be understood, in humanist manner, as the free individual being swayed by ideology. For Althusser, there is no essential core of irrepressible humanity in the individual. He regards ideology as ultimately constitutive. We are born into it, come to consciousness within it; it is confirmed, continually, in the practices of everyday life. Our subjectivities—the very idea that we *have* subjectivities—all this is constructed in ideology. Hence we recognize ourselves as the kinds of people ideology needs us to be. The social formation reproduces itself by constituting subjects who "work by themselves," says Althusser. There are "'bad subjects' who on occasion provoke the intervention of one of the detachments of the (repressive) State apparatus. But the vast majority of (good) subjects work all right 'all by themselves', that is, by ideology" (p. 169). So ideology does not deceive us, we discover our selves through it.

Now, this argument addresses powerfully the question of why there is not more dissidence, but at the cost of making it hard to see how there can be any dissidence at all. For if our subjectivities are constituted within a language and social system that is already imbued with oppressive constructs of class, race, gender, and sexuality, then how can we expect to see past that, to the idea of a fairer society, let alone struggle to achieve it? How, indeed, could Althusser see what he did?

At this point, new historicism converges on Althusser, with respect to its preoccupation with what I call the "entrapment model" of ideology and power. This model claims that even attempts to challenge the system help to maintain it; in fact, those attempts are distinctively complicit, insofar as they help the dominant to assert and police the boundaries of the deviant and the permissible. In the entrapment model, any move seems to have been anticipated by the power system—you only dig yourself in deeper. As Don Wayne puts it, new historicism has often shown "how different kinds of discourse intersect, contradict, destabilise, cancel, or modify each other . . . seek[ing] to demonstrate how a dominant ideology will give a certain rein to alternative discourses, ultimately appropriating their vitality and containing their oppositional force."[3] Dissidence plays into the hands of containment.

Attitudes toward the entrapment model constitute a principal effective difference between cultural materialism and new historicism. For west-European Marxism and cultural materialism, the importance of Althusser and the entrapment model was manifest, as a way of theorizing the power of dominant ideologies. Even more important, though, was theorizing a way out of that—theorizing the scope for dissidence. This, centrally, is what Raymond Williams was concerned with in his later work. In the 1950s Williams elaborated an influential socialist-humanist protest against the cultural degradation which he associated with capitalism. This protest was parallel with Frankfurt School work, but maintained also a belief in the validity of "lived experience" and an optimism about the potential of welfare-capitalism. After 1968, and specifically the inadequacies of the Labour administrations of 1964–70, Williams turned to the non-Stalinist Marxist tradition, in the writings of V.N. Volosinov and Antonio Gramsci, seeking a more theoretical and materialist understanding of ideology. Cultural materialism is his term.

In his essay "Base and Superstructure in Marxist Cultural Theory" (1973), Williams argued against the tendency in Marxist analysis to regard culture as a mere effect and reflection of the economic organization. He believed this tendency derived from an inadequate conception of the "productive forces" in society, overlooking "the primary production of society itself, and of men themselves, the material production and reproduction of real life." Thus far, Williams is close to Althusser, who in the course of just such an argument about the reproduction of people, posits "a 'relative autonomy' of the superstructure with respect to the base" and "a 'reciprocal action' of the superstructure on the base."[4] However, Williams turns then to Gramsci's work on hegemony as a way of analyzing not only the power of ideology as "deeply saturating the consciousness of a society," but also the scope for dissidence. "We have to emphasize that hegemony is not singular; indeed that its own internal structures are highly complex, and have continually to be renewed, recreated and defended; and by the same token, that they can be continuously challenged and in certain respects modified," says Williams (pp. 37–38). So while there is a "dominant culture"—"the central, effective and dominant systems of meanings and values, which are not merely abstract but which are organized and lived" (p. 38)—its dominance depends on continuous processes of adjustment, reinterpretation, incorporation, dilution. And, furthermore, these processes are conducted in relation to "alternative" and "oppositional," "residual" and "emergent" cultural formations (pp. 40–42). The dominant may tolerate, repress, or incorporate these other formations, but that will be a continuous, urgent, and often strenuous project.

The relevant elaboration of the theory of ideology in response to the challenge of Althusser and the entrapment model, then, is this: conflict and contradiction stem from the very strategies through which dominant ideologies strive to contain the expectations that they need to generate. Despite their power, dominant ideological formations are always, in practice, under pressure from diverse disturbances. These disturbances do not derive from our irrepressible humanity, but from pressures and strains which the social order inevitably produces within itself, even as it attempts to secure itself. The successes and failures of dissidence in our own situations, therefore, derive not from ineluctable laws, making compliance the condition of any human society, but from relative strengths and weaknesses in determinate historical circumstances.

In recent years the question of dissidence versus containment has often been approached through the work of Michel Foucault. He has been taken as the theorist of entrapment, and is often used to underwrite new historicist concerns. This is because he writes: "Where there is power, there is resistance, and yet, or rather consequently, this resistance is never in a position of exteriority in relation to power." However, Foucault was a committed and active leftist, and his project here has to be understood within the framework I have been identifying. When he says there is "no single locus of great Refusal, no soul of revolt, source of all rebellions, or pure law of the revolutionary," he is repudiating Marcuse's belief that the events of 1968 amounted to "the Great Refusal" and were grounds for anticipating the end of capitalist repression.[5] (Similarly, Foucault's insistence that sex is produced, rather than repressed, in our societies is formulated partly with reference to Marcuse's ideas of sexual liberation.) Like Althusser, Foucault rejects the idea of an essential core of irrepressible humanity; like the British left, he is trying to locate a credible theory of dissidence in the wake of such enthusiasms and disappointments. There is, he says, "a plurality of resistances." They are "distributed in irregular fashion: the points, knots, or focuses of resistance are spread over time and space at varying densities, at times mobilizing groups or individuals in a definitive way" (p. 96).

This argument does not, Foucault insists, imply an entrapment model: these resistances are not "only a reaction or rebound, forming with respect to the basic domination an underside that is in the end always passive, doomed to perpetual defeat." On the contrary, even a discourse of stigma may be thrown into a reverse signification. Homosexuality, says Foucault, was elaborated in nineteenth-century legal, medical, and sexological discourses, making possible new forms of control. But this very process gave a voice to sexual dissidence: "Homosexuality began to speak in its own behalf, to demand that its legitimacy or 'naturality' be acknowledged, often in the same vocabulary, using the same categories by which it was medically disqualified." Deviancy returns from abjection by deploying just those terms which relegated it in the first place. There may be "great radical ruptures," occasionally; but it is "the strategic codification of these points of resistance that makes a revolution possible."[6] This is an apposite message for the west-European left: there is no simple way through, but every reason to go on trying.

Art and Cultural Production

Despite their differences, Marcuse and Althusser both accord a uniquely privileged role to art. The Frankfurt School believed that the full humanity withheld from people under capitalism will obtrude nonetheless, though in oblique forms, as an intuition of utopia; and especially in the fullness of artworks. Fredric Jameson finds "the Utopian impulse" even in the representations of leisure-class people in Marcel Proust's *A la recherche du temps perdu*; he takes them to reflect "in the most distorted way the possibilities of a world in which alienated labour will have ceased to exist." Jameson grants that "the Proustian leisure class is a caricature of that classless society: how could it be otherwise? Yet since it is (at least in Proust's society) the only leisure culture which exists, it alone can serve as a source of concrete images of what such a Utopia might be like."[7] To which one might reply: If that's what utopia is going to be like, it's just as well we have plenty of time to think it over.

Althusser also accorded a special role to art and literature. It is not true, as at least two recent studies have asserted, that he thought of them as ideological state apparatuses. "*I do not rank real art among the ideologies,*" Althusser declares. Art "*alludes* to reality"; it "makes us *see* . . . the *ideology* from which it is born, in which it bathes, from which it detaches itself as art." It does this by effecting an "*internal distantiation.*" Through its formal properties, art draws attention to the ideology in which it is constructed; thus it occupies a distinctive position between ideology and Marxist knowledge.[8] This theory is anticipated by the Russian formalists and by Bertolt Brecht (in the *Verfremdumseffekt*), but Althusser derives it from Pierre Macherey's *Theory of Literary Production* (1966). Macherey argues that literary language "imitates the everyday language which is the language of ideology. We could offer a provisional definition of literature as being characterized by this power of parody. Mingling the real uses of language in an endless confrontation, it concludes by *revealing* their truth." Thus literature "*reveals* the gaps in ideology."[9] These ideas were very influential in the early phases of "theory" in Britain—for instance in Colin MacCabe's essay "Realism and the Cinema: Notes on Some

Brechtian Theses" (*Screen*, 1974), Terry Eagleton's *Criticism and Ideology* (1976), Terry Hawkes's *Structuralism and Semiotics* (1977), and Catherine Belsey's *Critical Practice* (1980).

The flaw in the ideas of Marcuse, Althusser, and Macherey, from a cultural materialist standpoint, is that they assume that we all know what art and literature are ("I mean authentic art, not works of an average or mediocre level," Althusser avers, unhelpfully). They carry over, virtually, the bourgeois-liberal notion. Marx, indeed, had done this, and most British socialists; the task, as they saw it, was to redefine the roles of an apparently-known entity—art—within a socialist theory.[10] There was a further, partly alternative, tradition concerned with folk art, working-class writing, and music hall, but it appeared fatally weakened by the mass media. Williams in *Culture and Society* (1958) refuses the idea of "proletarian" art, on the ground that "the traditional popular culture of England was, if not annihilated, at least fragmented and weakened by the dislocations of the Industrial Revolution," so that what remains "is small and narrow in range." He asserts the relevance of the central culture to everyone: "The body of intellectual and imaginative work which each generation receives as its traditional culture is always, and necessarily, something more than the product of a single class."[11] Everyone, therefore, is entitled to share privileges hitherto appropriated by the upper classes. This is the welfare-capitalist move.

"The crucial theoretical break," Williams wrote in 1977—and it was a break for him too, which made it additionally significant—"is the recognition of 'literature' as a specializing social and historical category." Macherey also came to see this, in an essay written with Etienne Balibar, in 1978.[12] In *Marxism and Literature*, Williams presents a history of literature that is not a historical situating of texts already-agreed to be literary, but a history of the concept "Literature," showing it to be the product of economic, social, and political changes running through from the eighteenth century. Insistence on the processes through which a text achieves its current estimation is the key move in cultural materialism, and a principal difference in emphasis from new historicism.

For not all societies have art and literature. Very many value specially some objects and texts, usually in relation to religious and social hierarchies, and most ornament and elaborate some objects and texts far beyond usefulness. But they do not regard them as "art" and "literature." To be sure, we have assimilated to our concepts diverse objects and texts from those other cultures—religious paintings are put into galleries, churches become artworks. But that is our doing. Literature is not an objective category of value, but a discourse we have been constructing—in order to assert, and contest, certain ranges of value in our cultures. Marx, famously, wondered why ancient Greek art remains potent for us; is it not an instance of art transcending historical conditions? Marx (evidently at a loss) thought it might be because the Greeks lived in "the historic childhood of humanity" and hence exercise "an eternal charm."[13] Cultural materialists say: Greek art is valued while we find it useful as a way of handling our own dilemmas and maintain an ongoing discourse that appropriates it. Actually, of course, the classics haven't been lasting so well lately. If you raise the question of the Greeks with students today you probably get: So . . . erm . . . which Greeks were those, exactly? That is because most people have found more convenient bodies of work—other writings— around which to conduct current cultural contests.

A reappraisal of operations then follows. When we ask: What are the truly literary qualities? we should ask also: Who says these are literary qualities, and why? Not just: What is it about this text that makes it literary? but: What is it in the social organization that makes some people regard this text as literary? Literature becomes one set of practices within the range of cultural production; a "discourse," we might say, meaning the working assumptions of those involved in those practices, together with the institutions that sustain them. Notions of literature transcending society, history, and politics then appear, in themselves, as ideological maneuvers. And study of literature, like study of other modes of cultural production, will attend to how it functions in the social order   considering the kinds of human possibilities that it promotes, and may be made to promote; how it acts to sustain the prevailing power relations, and affords opportunity for dissidence and new understanding.

For many younger Englit academics, this reappraisal offered an exciting prospect. The expansion of higher education in the 1960s, we may now see, allowed into humanities teaching too many bright, upwardly-mobile people, who passed tests in Englit (we knew who wanted his pound of flesh), but whose class background had not conferred on them an inbred sensitivity to art; and whose student culture was organized, typically, around cinema, beat poetry, rock music, and the peace movement. At first this disjunction didn't notice too much, because the old guard was still very much in charge, because academia was becoming more of a profession and less of a gentlemanly hobby anyway, and because we worked hard at ventriloquizing establishment culture. This mimicry was often uncomfortable, producing a self-division between the initial class culture of family and neighborhood, the student culture of electronic reproduction and political activism, and the old, establishment culture. But we accepted, by and large, a Marcusean cultural politics: modern societies inhibit creativity, literature is creative, and so social progress means (among other things) having more literature.

Political disappointments, focused by the events of 1968, made this increasingly inadequate. Then, suddenly, the Women's Movement showed that the alleged universality of quality culture was, in large part, male presumption. In 1979, within a decade of Germaine Greer's *Female Eunuch* and Kate Millett's *Sexual Politics*, Elaine Showalter distinguished two kinds of currently burgeoning work. One kind considers how "the hypothesis of a female reader changes our apprehension of a given text, awakening us to the significance of its sexual codes"; the other investigates "woman as the producer of textual meaning."[14] It is salutary to recall, now, how far such topics were from customary critical procedures. Feminism created space for other kinds of question. We saw that we didn't, after all, have to spend our psychic energy on ever more ingenious explanations of why Shakespeare on Shylock, or Joseph Conrad on Blacks, or D.H. Lawrence on women, or Alexander Pope on Sporus and effeminacy, is really expressing a profound universal truth.

Drawing attention to such instances provoked violent and irrational responses in the establishment, so we knew we were onto something. From here, one route was into Cultural Studies. Initially this meant working-class culture, past and present; it was pursued notably by upwardly mobile boys who had been doing their schoolwork while the other kids were hanging out on the block, and consequently had made it through the academic system. They turned back from the sissified high-cultural tradition, toward the rough boys who had harassed them on their way home from school; somewhat romantically, they wondered how far such behavior might amount to a form of resistance. From this vein, Stuart Hall and his associates at the Centre for Contemporary Cultural Studies at the University of Birmingham quarried principal themes and theories in cultural materialism. The other route was to hang on and hijack Englit, enjoying the aggro and believing that it is a significant site of struggle. In fact, the choice of text doesn't matter nearly as much as what you do with it; the history of literary criticism shows, conclusively, that it is all too common to be stupid and insensitive about *King Lear*, and quite possible to be generous and thoughtful about *Some Like It Hot*.

The Politics of Literature

In the first enthusiasm of political criticism, literature and Shakespeare especially were deplored by some as the conduit of everything reactionary —capital, patriarchy, nation, and empire. After all, Margaret Thatcher's chancellor, Nigel Lawson, did co-opt Shakespeare as "a Tory, without any doubt," on the basis of Ulysses's order speech in *Troilus and Cressida* and "the Tory virtues, the Roman virtues" in *Coriolanus*.[15] Shakespeare is widely used in politics and the heritage business to signify Englishness; he's what the English have left to feel proud about.

However, the idea that literature is promoted in order to strengthen the forces of reaction is too close to Althusser, in the sense of assuming too much ideological coherence and purpose. As Williams observes, classes are not culturally monolithic. Within them, groups may be rising or falling, and there may be alternative affiliations, in religion or sexuality for instance, that are not characteristic of the class as a whole; they produce class fractions (Williams discusses William Godwin and his circle, the pre-Raphaelites and Bloomsbury).[16] In fact, although literary culture has often been broadly complicit with establishment values, we don't actually expect our rulers, in business, government, or the military, to have a sensitive apprehension of literary values; usually they despise them. Literature has often been a dissident formation, of a particular kind. Since the late eighteenth century, when the French Revolution, land enclosures, the factory system, and urbanization helped to stimulate the Romantic movement, the middle class has thrown up a dissident fraction partly hostile to the hegemony of that class. The line runs through the pre-Raphaelites, the decadent and aesthetic movements, Fabianism, Bloomsbury, modernism, public- (i.e., private-) school communists, Leavisism, various new lefts, feminisms, peace movements, the green movement. In conjunction with such middle-class, dissident movements, art and literature have been constituted (along with the spirit, nature, personal religion, intimate and family relations) as "the human," in a broad opposition to mechanical, urban, industrial and commercial organization in the modern world. Middle-class dissidence sets culture against the brutality of the system.

The weakness of this dissidence is that it starts from an acknowledgment of the priority of the utilitarian analysis as the first term in the argument. It accepts that art is no good at addressing the real world of material affairs (that's why it is provocative to say that Shakespeare is political); art, it says, is the special province of the human, the spiritual, the personal. Thus it accepts the binary opposition that includes its own sub-ordination. And, by so much, it is discouraged from addressing the main determinants of events, which are not the human, the spiritual and the personal, but the institutional power of big business, the military, and government. Nevertheless, middle-class dissidence has been and is a valid political formation in its own right, and it is a mistake to imagine that political rectitude is the prerogative of more obviously oppressed groups.

The embarrassment of middle-class cultural dissidence is that it is gendered; there is something "feminine" about it. "Manliness" is cele-brated as the inspiration of industry, business, the military, and empire; and art finds itself, in counterpart, in a feminine stance. When Hermann Goering reaches for his gun, we reach for our culture. Consider Matthew Arnold's phraseology: he sets humanist sweetness and light against the philistines and the barbarians. The latter two may be vulgar, but they do sound like real men. Tennessee Williams found writing a refuge when he was young—"From being called a sissy by the neighborhood kids, and Miss Nancy by my father, because I would rather read books in my grand-father's large and classical library than play marbles and baseball and other normal kid games."[17] Literary dissidence accepts—in the main very gingerly—a touch of the feminine. Its invocation of a "human" protest depends on a strategic deployment of effeminacy: of culture against brutal-ity, the spirit against the system, style against purpose, personal emotion against compulsion. Hence the commonplace that the great writer is an-drogynous. There musn't be too much of the "wrong" sex, though. The trick in artistic dissidence is to appropriate sufficient of the radical aura of androgyny, without more than is necessary of the disabling stigma. The great writer embraces something of the feminine, it is often said—but not too much.

None of this has been to the advantage of women. Effeminacy, as I said in the previous chapter, is a misogynist construct whereby the sexu-ality of men is policed through the accusation of sliding back from the purposeful reasonableness that is supposed to constitute manliness, into the laxity and weakness conventionally attributed to women. Englit and literary culture have depended on an effeminacy which they also need to disavow, and hence the derogation of the writing and reading of women. In the eighteenth and nineteenth centuries, women were regarded as the natural producers of culture; it seemed an extension of their domestic and nurturing responsibilities. They contributed hugely to imaginative writing and, as the larger body of readers, arbitrated upon literary taste. The fashionable mid-nineteenth century writer Nathaniel Willis observed: "It is the women who read. It is the women who are the tribunal of any question aside from politics or business. It is the women who give or withhold a literary reputation."[18] Again, more enthusiastically: "literature," Jessie Boucherette remarked, "is followed, as a profession, by women, to an extent far greater than our readers are at the moment aware of. Magazines of the day are filled by them; one of the oldest and best of our weekly periodicals owes two-thirds of its content to their pens." As Mary Poovey comments, even if such opinions were not wholly accurate, it is important that they were "widely held."[19] The access of women to literary culture "was due of course to the extreme cheapness of its professional requirements," Virginia Woolf noted. "Books, pens and paper are so cheap, reading and writing have been, since the eighteenth century at least, so universally taught in our class, that it was impossible for any body of men to corner the necessary knowledge or to refuse admittance, except on their own terms, to those who wished to read books or to write them."[20]

Through the nineteenth century, there was a spate of awkward male repudiations and negotiations. Charles Kingsley—author of *The Water Babies*—in his "Thoughts on Shelley and Byron" (1853) declared that "the age" is "an effeminate one," and that this may be seen from the popular preference for Shelley over Byron. Kingsley finds in Byron "the sturdy peer proud of his bull neck and his boxing, who kept bears and bull-dogs, drilled Greek ruffians at Missolonghi, and 'had no objection to a pot of beer'"; all this went, it seems, with a strong sense of moral law. Of course, we know now that Byron had sexual relations with both women and men; the point is not what he did or didn't do, but the need for literary culture to set boundaries between itself and the unacceptably effeminate. The bad opposite of Byron, in Kingsley's view, is Shelley: his nature "is utterly womanish. Not merely his weak points, but his strong ones, are those of a woman. Tender and pitiful as a woman; and yet, when angry, shrieking, railing, hysterical as a woman. The physical distaste for meat and fermented liquors, coupled with the hankering after physical horrors, are especially feminine."[21] It is in the nature of such disavowals that they must continually be repeated. Often it was asserted that only false literature is feminine; in 1870 Alfred Austin lamented that whereas great art is "manly," those were "feminine, timorous, narrow, domesticated" times, and hence inclined to produce feminine poetry.[22]

Part of the project of literary modernism, as Sandra M. Gilbert and Susan Gubar have shown, was to repudiate nineteenth-century forbears generally as effeminate. T.E. Hulme complained that "imitative poetry springs up like weeds, and women whimper and whine of you and I alas, and roses, roses all the way. It becomes the expression of sentimentality rather than of virile thought."[23] Henry James, Ann Douglas points out, felt he had to insist "to the reading public, and himself, that fiction, the traditional province of women, be accorded all the seriousness of history, the customary province of men."[24] However, the boundary still could not be secured; the symbolist vein runs through—observe, for instance, the critical difficulty in deciding at what point W.B. Yeats's poetry becomes acceptably "modern."

The anxiety about effeminacy was exacerbated by the wish to establish English Literature as the kind of thing that might properly be studied in universities. If it was soppy, girls' stuff, you couldn't plausibly offer it as an academic discipline. This, I suggest, was the abiding factor in the maneuverings of literary criticism in the first half of this century. Irving Babbitt lamented in 1908 that "men of business" regard poetry as "a pretty enough thing for our wives and daughters" while men take science courses and women literary courses. The latter, "indeed, are known in some of these institutions as 'sissy' courses. The man who took literature too seriously would be suspected of effeminacy. The really virile thing to be is an electrical engineer. One already sees the time when the typical teacher of literature will be some young dilettante who will interpret Keats and Shelley to a class of girls."[25] Babbitt found that "the more vigorous and pushing teachers of language feel that they must assert their manhood by philological research"—though this was unnecessary, he believed, because the true humanist makes "a vigorous and virile application of ideas to life," his mind being "assimilative in the active and masculine sense" (119, 133, 135). In England, the project of F.R. Leavis was to make literature fit for a man to study. Once again, Shelley comes off badly. He is accused of "tender, caressing, voluptuous effects," and of "the conventional bathos of album poeticizing, not excluding banalities about . . . the sad lot of woman." Leavis's not-Shelley is Wordsworth: he evinces "emotional discipline, critical exploration of his experience, pondered valuation and maturing reflection."[26] Much more manly; but the distinction is still not very safe. "I wandered lonely as a cloud / That floats on high o'er vales and hills": William Wordsworth. It's nice, but not all *that* manly.

Professional Englit systematically disqualified or ignored all but a few women authors. In the view of the men who dominated Englit, this was a small price for keeping imputations of effeminacy at bay. By the 1970s, when feminists challenged orthodox assumptions, it seemed that women had contributed little of significance to writing. These days we have theory, which of course is really hunky. Harold Bloom, for instance, imagines literature passing from father to son in an Oedipal romance uncontaminated by female mediation.

The thought that literature is unmanly has been more worrying and more marked in the United States because of the frontier tradition; it is un-American not to be manly. Further, writers are reckoned to have contributed in a major way to the whole idea of being "American." "The American has a duty beyond and above that of inventing an anti-classical form," William Carlos Williams wrote, "that of honoring his country and its language"—of making "Americans" from diverse peoples.[27] Walt Whitman seemed to have got it right in the nineteenth century: he celebrated a "manly love" that invoked both the frontier tradition and the prospect of a democratic future. In fact, Whitman virtually made poetry possible for "Americans" (as Hemingway was to do with the novel). To Whitmanians, Leslie Fiedler explained in 1964, "being American means despising the culture of Europe, indeed, all high culture, finally the very notion of culture itself."[28]

Even so, the question about whether Whitman had "feminine traits" had been raised, for instance by Havelock Ellis in his *Sexual Inversion* (1897). Ellis's principal witness was John Addington Symonds—who, not content with hijacking Shakespeare's *Venus and Adonis*, had tried for eighteen years to get Whitman to admit that there is sexual love between men in his Calamus poems. The evidence appears inconclusive. Consider this letter from an associate of Whitman, which Ellis prints: "I knew Walt Whitman personally. To me Mr. Whitman was one of the most robust and virile of men, extraordinarily so. He was from my standpoint not feminine at all, but physically masculine and robust. The difficulty is that a virile and strong man who is poetic in temperament, ardent and tender, may have phases and moods of passion and emotion which are apt to be misinterpreted."[29] Observe the difficulty: insofar as Whitman is poetic, he IS effeminate, after all—but not, of course, in an unmanly way.

These anxieties became unavoidable with the popularization of psychoanalysis in the mid-twentieth century. Mark van Doren attacked Whitman in 1935 in an essay, "Walt Whitman, Stranger"—the title already has the poet cast out from the community of decent "Americans." Whitman has appeared "robust and masculine, a representative male," van Doren says. But actually he was "fastidious, eccentric and feminine," too interested in clothes, and given to wearing "shirts with lace-edged collars, opening on a fine neck which he regularly bathed with eau de cologne and which he set off with a large pearl. He was a good cook, and during the Civil War, of course, he was a nurse. So, as time has gone on, he has been recognized as the inverted individual that in one degree or another he was. . . . There would be no good reason for speaking of this," van Doren adds, "were it not that Whitman has been at such pains to put himself forward as a representative or normal American."[30] That was the rub: the very writers who seemed to have created America had in fact been un-American—subversives planting queer passions in the American identity.

President Kennedy told his countrymen and women: "we have thought of the artist as an idler and a dilettante and of the lover of the arts as somehow sissy or effete. We have done both an injustice."[31] Kennedy didn't mean that it is all right to be sissy and effete, but that art has been wrongly linked to all that. Hence the notoriety of Allen Ginsberg, who takes up the Whitman manner while refusing to accept that either homosexuality or communism is shameful. "It's true I don't want to join the Army," he writes, but "America I'm putting my queer shoulder to the wheel."[32] That was not what America had expected or wanted. And it doesn't want people like Ginsberg in the army.

Texts and Silences

Thus far I have considered mainly how the cultural materialist will address cultural institutions. He or she will be equally interested in reading texts. The traditional practice of Englit—in fact its virtual *raison d'être*—has been helping the text into an acceptable coherence by supplying feasible ways of smoothing over gaps and silences. If the words scripted for Hamlet or Iago seem not to explain their actions to the satisfaction of the modern reader, you can imagine aspects of their characters that will help them into sense. If push comes to shove, and the poet says something right over the top, such as "'Beauty is truth, truth beauty,'—that is all / Ye know on earth, and all ye need to know," you can declare that Keats didn't really mean it, he was using irony and paradox.

It is axiomatic in cultural materialism, as generally in poststructuralist theory, that no text, literary or otherwise, can contain within its project all the potential significance that it must release in pursuance of that project.

Closure is always inadequate. The complexity of the social formation and the multiaccentuality of language combine to produce an inevitable excess of meaning. Macherey theorized this back in 1966. "When we explain the work, instead of ascending to a hidden centre which is the source of life (the interpretive fallacy is organicist and vitalist), we perceive its actual decentred-ness. . . . The literary work gives the measure of a difference, reveals a determinate absence, resorts to an eloquent silence."[33] It is a technical point, almost: every inside is defined by its outside. The text cannot be self-sufficient, an ideal whole. Without gaps, silences, and absences—that which the text is not—it would not exist; they frame it. They inform us of "the precise conditions for the appearance of an utterance, and thus its limits, giving its real significance" (p. 86). This argument is continuous with the one about how ideology cannot but allow dissidence: all stories comprise within themselves the ghosts of the alternative stories they are trying to suppress.

This theory licenses two cultural materialist procedures. First, it supersedes traditional forms of the text/context dichotomy. History, Macherey shows us, is not in an external relation to the work; "it is present in the work, in so far as the emergence of the work required this history, which is its only principle of reality" (p. 93).

> Thus, it is not a question of introducing a historical explanation which is stuck onto the work from outside. On the contrary, we must show a sort of splitting within the work: this division is *its* unconscious, in so far as it possesses one—the unconscious which is history, the play of history beyond its edges, encroaching on those edges: this is why it is possible to trace the path which leads from the haunted work to that which haunts it. (p. 94)

The problem with this formulation is that Macherey is inclined still, at this date, to counterpose literature and history (or ideology); "the reverse side of what is written will be history itself," he adds. Cultural materialism generally goes one stage further, arguing (1) that any text may be read deconstructively, and (2) that everything is "history itself."

Second, Macherey legitimates readings that will not respect the ostensive project of the text. It is not a matter of catching out the author, he insists: "the work is not at fault in relation to another work in which the absences would be made good, the insufficiencies remedied" (p. 128). True; but in a context where one's colleagues are asserting that Shakespeare has a profound intuitive insight into what love between women and men is really about, it is provocative to observe that Olivia in *Twelfth Night* falls improbably silent at just the moment when anything she might plausibly say would disrupt the normalizing patriarchal closure at the end of that play. Or, when it is widely supposed that Macbeth's rule of Scotland represents an aberrant refusal of "natural" socio-political relations, it is provocative to observe that the Scottish state is as violent under its "good" and "legitimate" monarchs as it is under the usurper.[34] The silences of the text manifest moments at which its ideological project is under special strain. For as Nicos Poulantzas observes, "ideology has the precise function of hiding the real contradictions and of *reconstituting* on an imaginary level a relatively coherent discourse."[35] Traditionally, critics read for coherence; cultural materialists read for incoherence. Macherey anticipates this approach in his essay on Tolstoy. If the text may be said to be a mirror, he says, it is a selective one. "The mirror selects, it does not reflect everything. The selection itself is not fortuitous, it is symptomatic; it can tell us about the nature of the mirror. We already know the reasons for this selectivity; Tolstoy's version of his age is incomplete because of his personal and ideological relation to it" (p. 120).

Cultural materialists say that canonical texts have political projects, and should not be allowed to circulate in the world today on the assumption that their representations of class, race, ethnicity, gender and sexuality are simply authoritative. We don't mind texts having political projects, of course; we believe that every representation, with its appeal for recognition —It is like *this*, isn't it?—is political. But we think the politics should be up for discussion, and that textual analysis should address it. In the next chapter I apply some of these ideas to Tennessee Williams and his context.

A Handy Test for Manliness?

In the meantime, men of letters may be reassured to hear of a tidy test for manliness—according to Havelock Ellis and other early sexologists. "The frequent inability of male inverts to whistle was first pointed out by Ulrichs," Ellis says, "and Hirschfield has found it in 23 percent. Many of my cases confess to this inability." "Inverted women," conversely, "are very often good whistlers; Hirschfield even knows two who are public performers in whistling."[36] John Addington Symonds, the hijacker of *Venus and Adonis*, took up the idea: "My muscular build was slight, I could not throw a ball or stone like other boys. And, oddly enough, I could not learn to whistle like them. And yet I was by no means effeminate." In *Antony and Cleopatra*, our manly hero finds himself stood up by Cleopatra: "Antony, / Enthron'd i' the market place, did sit alone, / Whistling to the air."[37] He was a real man (there may be a research topic here).

Unfortunately the test is not altogether reliable. For instance, Ellis's case-history F.R. (I don't think this can be F.R. Leavis): "His tastes are chiefly of a literary character, and he has never had any liking for sports"; he thinks he has "a feminine mind in a male body." Yet F.R. "is able to whistle" (p. 95). It just won't add up. Then there is T.D. At the age of ten he formed attachments to other boys, he says, such as "Shelley speaks of as preceding love in ardent natures." Now, Shelley of course is a suspicious character, so no wonder T.D. grew up to "derive great pleasure from all literary and pictorial art and architecture," show "facility in writing per- sonal lyrical verse," and love other guys. Yet T.D. "can whistle easily and well" (pp. 118–19). Even so, Ellis evidently thinks, it would be a pity to relinquish the idea. After all, Shelley, no less, "was unable to whistle, though he never gave an indication of inversion; but he was a person of somewhat abnormal and feminine organisation . . ." (p. 291).

3. Un-American Activities

During World War II, U.S. recruiting officers were on the look out for two unmanly types: malingerers and homosexuals. The malingerers were drafted, but gays were rejected; whatever they did, they couldn't be manly. But what of the gay man who tried really hard to get into the services? Was that not *prima facie* evidence of manly courage? No, he was rejected, and there was a special term for him: *reverse malingerer*.[1] It was unthinkable that he might actually be brave and "American"; however hard he tried to enlist, he must be some kind of malingerer. He was a "reverse malingerer," lacking the potential even of true malingerers. Such ideological pressure may explain why President Clinton reneged on allowing lesbians and gay men to present themselves openly in the military. In this chapter I attempt to demonstrate, refine and extend some practices and principles in cultural politics and subcultural reading.

Latent Un-Americans

Wartime disturbance of conventional patterns of and attitudes toward sexual behaviors incited quasi-expert attention to homosexuality. Psychoanalyst Gustav Bychowski, in an article called "The Ego of Homosexuals" (1945), attributes every kind of "feminine" weakness to male homosexuals. Despite this, though, they are dangerous. "The ego-feeling of these individuals should not be judged by their behaviour. They are impertinent, possessive, cocksure," Bychowski says.[2] So they are men to be reckoned with, it seems; they defy social norms if they can get away with it. Nevertheless, they aren't really brave: "closer analysis reveals that their attitude and their ego-feeling are only a reaction formation against a deeply-seated feeling of weakness and insecurity" (p. 125). But then again, despite this underlying feebleness, they may be pugnacious. One actually wants to "fight for equality of rights for himself as identified with other wronged, frustrated and exploited individuals." For Bychowski, this is pathological and needs explanation: "Thus he used not only to gratify his narcissistic grandeur but also to better his own feelings of weakness and frustration" (p. 117).

The Cold War made it specially necessary to control sexual dissidence for, even more than battle conditions, it depended on the ideological—spiritual, moral—determination of U.S. people. They had to establish and maintain the superiority of "the American way of life" over communism. Un-Americans were dismissed from jobs in government, municipalities, business, education, and medicine, often on suspicion and without appeal. By the mid-1950s, one in five of the workforce had been required to sign an oath of moral purity in order to get or retain employment. Communists seemed to threaten military and political security; queers (I use the word of the time) undermined family values and the frontier vision of the manly man. Not that the convergence produced much solidarity. Audre Lorde was moving in "progressive circles" in 1953, but there "being gay was 'bourgeois and reactionary', a reason for suspicion and shunning. Besides, it made you 'more susceptible to the FBI'."[3]

I use "American" to signal an ideological construct—an imperial ideology, as we may easily discern in the way "American" subsumes the continent into the nation state (as if one said "Europe" to mean "Germany"). These "American values"—a tiny selection, it is important to remember, from the achievement and potential of U.S. people—were taken as the one proper range of human action and meaning by very many sociologists and psychoanalysts. These disciplines were dominated by functionalism, which views societies as integrated, harmonious wholes, wherein all parts function to maintain equilibrium, consensus and social order. This theory has obvious conservative consequences: everything is already in its place; change is not required, indeed it can hardly be envisaged. Factors that seem not to contribute to stability were termed "dysfunctional" by R.K. Merton; but often they were found to be satisfactory after all (e.g., critical intellectuals help to keep the system alert).[4] The sociological argument was often couched in terms of the health of a social organism, and this fitted well with psychoanalysis, which declared the nuclear family and conventional gender roles to be the one, natural way to develop happy, healthy, productive people. Queers, conversely, were dysfunctional. Abram Kardiner, a prominent psychoanalyst, perceived in 1954 an "enormous" increase in homosexuality, and regarded it as "a symptom that the society is not functioning properly"; it was jeopardizing "social structure and social functioning," and was "a symptom of grave social dislocation."[5]

It was only a small step to the thought that anyone who didn't fit in was implicitly queer. Noting the "premium on self-assertion" in U.S. culture, Lionel Ovesey feared that "any adaptive failure—sexual, social, or vocational—may be perceived unconsciously as a failure in the masculine role," leading to the equation: "I am a failure = I am castrated = I am not a man = I am a woman = I am a homosexual." Since most of these "adaptive failures" seemed not, in fact, to engage in homosexual practices, Ovesey proposed for them the term "pseudo-homosexuals."[6]

The threat of being regarded as any kind of queer should have been marvelous at getting men to conform. It was reinforced by the idea of latency. Freud had thought there was an initial disposition towards bisexuality in every child: "Analysis shows that in every case a homosexual object-tie was present and in most cases persisted in a *latent* condition."[7] Latency meant that *anyone* might be subject to deep-set homosexual inclinations. This was convenient for witchhunters—it offered endless opportunities and required no sexual acts to be uncovered; being alleged to have a "tendency" was sufficient to justify an undesirable discharge from the army.[8] In fact, latency was too good; once you started looking, no one was exempt.

This problem was augmented by the Kinsey Reports. *Sexual Behavior in the Human Male* (1948) suggested that all kinds of illicit sexual activity were far more widespread than most people had supposed, and specially male homosexuality. The implications were recognized to be un-American. "Kinsey's erroneous conclusions pertaining to homosexuality will be politically and propagandistically used against the United States abroad, stigmatizing the nation as a whole in a whisper campaign," declared Edmund Bergler, a leading psychoanalyst, in 1954.[9] Cold War U.S. culture wanted latency—that is why it went on about it. It was the most far-reaching way of worrying about manliness. That culture also did not want latency—it was too uncomfortable. How could communism be defeated if so many Americans were un-American? Latency is a faultline story.

This anxiety structures Arthur Miller's play, *A View from the Bridge* (1955–56). Eddie collects indications that Rodolpho might be latently queer and kisses him as an insult, thereby arousing suspicions in many audiences and readers that Eddie himself is latently queer. The point is not whether either of them is or ever has been, but the power of the undecidable accusation and fear. As with *The Crucible*, this makes *A View from the Bridge* an analogue of McCarthyism. However, it is hardly a courageous one since, as John Clum points out, the "rightness" of the play's dénouement depends on Eddie's opinion about Rodolpho being mistaken; it is not all right for the boy actually to be gay.[10] The good and authoritative narrator, Alfieri, announces a generally conservative view of sex and gender roles: "I'm warning you—the law is nature. The law is only a word for what has a right to happen. When the law is wrong it's because it's unnatural, but in this case it is natural."[11] In fact, it is this belief in conventional sex and gender roles, which all the characters share, that causes the trouble; but you have to read against the grain to get such a thought. It is important also, I think, that the action is set in an immigrant community: once these people have become properly American they won't carry on in such passionate ways.

It became very necessary to distance yourself from latent homosexuality. In an article first published in 1954, Norman Mailer displays this beautifully. He acknowledges, as a result of reading Donald Webster Cory's *The Homosexual in America* (1951), that he has been wrong to be so prejudiced against homosexuals. As a result, Mailer feels he understands "more about people, more about life." There is "another benefit. There is probably no sensitive heterosexual alive who is not preoccupied at one time or another with his latent homosexuality, and while I had no conscious homosexual desires, I had wondered more than once if really there were not something suspicious in my intense dislike of homosexuals." One effect of his new self-analysis, Mailer suggests, is to exculpate him: now he is so *unbothered* that he can contemplate the possibility of his own latent proclivity. He found he was "no longer concerned with latent homosexuality. It seemed vastly less important, and paradoxically enabled me to realize that I am actually quite heterosexual."[12] However, there is no winning with latency. The more you think you haven't got it, the more you might have it. After all, why does Mailer need to tell us all this? Perhaps we have been wondering about him; now we might wonder about why he needs to reassure himself and us.

Irving Bieber headed a group of psychoanalysts who were determined to extricate Americans—other than un-American Americans, of course—from such imputations. To this end, they were prepared even to repudiate parts of their Freudian heritage. Freud's notion of a general initial bisexuality allowed the inference that homosexuality was natural and hence healthy. Bieber and his crew would not have this. "All *psychoanalytic* theories assume that adult homosexuality is psychopathologic," they asserted, falsely.[13] And Freud was wrong about latency: "since the concept of homosexual latency is one that assumes a universal tendency present in all

men, we prefer to discard the term entirely." Thus they could conclude
that "heterosexuality is the *biologic* norm and that unless interfered with all
individuals are heterosexual." The infection of queerness could be isolated,
therefore, and even treated: Bieber &c. thought they could cure homosexuals through analysis (p. 319).

Nevertheless, the difficulty would not go away. By comparing homosexual and heterosexual patients, Bieber and his crew claim to have isolated
the pathological family background of the gay man. However, their figures
reveal something else. Of the homosexual group, 81 percent said their
mothers were dominating and 57 percent said they were seductive. But of
the heterosexual comparison group, 65 percent and 34 percent said this
too! More of the gays were persuaded to report dominating and seductive
mothers, but a high proportion of the heterosexual men had been deprived
of normative development by these allegedly monstrous women. Worse,
there was a dreadful inevitability about it, because the dominant and
seductive mothers were complemented by inadequate fathers. Of the gay
patients, 44 percent said their fathers humiliated them, and 56 percent said
they feared physical injury from their fathers. But of the comparison
group, the heterosexual patients, 40 percent said their fathers humiliated
them, and 43 percent that they feared physical injury from their fathers
(pp. 86–87). A whole cycle of male failure was revealed. Innumerable boys
were being humiliated and beaten by inadequate, presumptively heterosexual, American men. Of the homosexuals, 62 percent said their mothers
tried to ally with them against their fathers, and 58 percent said their
mothers openly preferred them to their fathers—not surprisingly, we
might think, given how unpleasant the fathers seemed to be. Of the comparison group, 40 percent gave the same reply to the first question, and 38
percent to the second. And while 64 percent of the homosexuals considered their mothers to be frigid, so did 47 percent of the heterosexuals
(p. 45). This was the scandal, then: the queer family was an intensified
version of the American family.

Furthermore, many of the supposedly heterosexual comparison
group exhibited suspiciously queer symptoms. They "revealed that they
feared homosexuals and homosexuality and that they had experienced
homosexual fantasies and dreams." Other relevant criteria were thought to
be the frequency with which the patient reported advances "by known or
suspected homosexuals," and whether he had ever wanted to be a woman.
Adding it all up, the results were disconcerting. Although 41 percent of the
heterosexuals surveyed had "no problem," 17 percent reported a "mild

problem," 15 percent a "moderate problem," and 27 percent a "severe problem" (p. 258). This was awkward: how could homosexuality be purged from the American psyche if over half the comparison group experienced it as a problem—a "severe" problem in a quarter of the instances?

"Naming it Dirty": Open Secrets

Tennessee Williams's plays show all too many signs of Cold War Freudian thinking, especially about American women. It made them out to be fragile, deluded, and dangerous; subject to hysterical sexual repression, which rendered them alternately frigid and nymphomaniac. They clung on to their children, blighting their sexual potential, and, given a chance, tried to humiliate the men they should respect. Therefore they might be patronized and if necessary raped; either way they had to be kept in their place. Nevertheless, in certain plays Williams suggests more adventurous possibilities, offering the opportunity and the risk that dissident strategies often admit: disturbing certain orthodoxies at the expense of admitting other regressive implications.

Latent homosexuality is the question around Brick and Skipper in Williams's *Cat on a Hot Tin Roof* (1955). Brick claims the innocent manly love of the frontier tradition: "Not love with you, Maggie, but friendship with Skipper was that one great true thing." Maggie says she accepts this: "Brick, I tell you, you got to believe me, Brick, I *do* understand all about it! I—I think it was—*noble*! Can't you tell I'm sincere when I say I respect it?" But the more she insists, the worse it sounds—that is the double bind of latency. Maggie is "naming it dirty," Brick says. She replies: "I know, believe me I know, that it was only Skipper that harbored even any *unconscious* desire for anything not perfectly pure between you two!"[14] Once unconscious desires are on the agenda, no one is beyond suspicion. And Brick is immature: he seems to have been over-mothered (pp. 66, 136, 142), and doesn't communicate well with his father (p. 90). He has problems with work and women, and is trying to hang on to his athletic youth. Now he won't sleep with Maggie, and his protestations of innocence are, of course, likely symptoms of latency.

Cleverly, Williams extends the provocation by making Brick declare that the relationship with Skipper was *not normal*. "No!—It was too rare to be normal, any true thing between two people is too rare to be normal." And he makes Brick acknowledge that when they were touring and shared rooms perhaps "we'd reach across the space between the two beds and shake hands to say goodnight, yeah, one or two times we—." The sentence is unfinished.[15] Williams makes Brick tease himself, and the perhaps anxious men in the audience, with the possibility of latent tendencies—or "homosexual problems," or "pseudo-homosexuality," or whatever it was to be called. After all, Skipper is distinctly suspect—he didn't make it in bed with Maggie, "thought it *was* true," and went to pieces (p. 123). As in *A View from the Bridge*, the two characters evidence two degrees of implication. In one aspect, Skipper's guilt exonerates Brick; in another, it drags him down.

For others in the play—and this was challenging in 1955—repression and social constraints, not homosexuality, are the problem. Maggie suggests that Skipper and Brick might have been fuller people if they had been queerer: "it couldn't be anything else, you being you, and that's what made it so sad, that's what made it so awful, because it was love that never could be carried through to anything satisfying or even talked about plainly" (p. 57). And Big Daddy, the unassailable patriarch who is both a frontiersman and a successful businessman, hates his wife, and thinks more of the male couple who owned the plantation before him and slept in the double bed on the stage—whose overseer and then partner he once was (pp. 116–17). In Big Daddy's experience, the frontier spirit is compatible with homosexuality. "I knocked around in my time . . . Slept in hobo jungles and railroad Y's and flophouses in all cities . . . I seen all things and understood a lot of them" (pp. 115–16). But this casual attitude has become untenable: the play recognizes, in 1955, a historical break. Unlike his father, Brick is profoundly frightened. "Big Daddy, you shock me, Big Daddy, you, you—*shock* me! Talkin' so—[*He turns away from his father.*]—casually!—about a—thing like that" (p. 119). And Brick has reason, in his experience, to be frightened: "Don't you know how people *feel* about things like that? How, how *disgusted* they are by things like that?" When in his fraternity a boy "*attempted* to do a, unnatural thing . . . We told him to git off the campus, and he did, he got" (p. 119). He was last heard of in North Africa, which is about as un-American as you can get.

Meanwhile, the older son, Gooper, is presented as a mature and responsible family man—but a dummy. With five children and one on the way and a career as a lawyer, he can claim to have secured the family inheritance. But the children are all awful and Gooper is dominated by his wife. Neither brother is going to achieve an unproblematic manliness; that has gone, with the earlier generations of men—straight and otherwise—

who built up the plantation. The double bed on the stage sets the failure of Brick's relationship with Maggie against the idea of the homosexual couple who once slept in it. Men lose their grip when they get caught up in the modern American family, the play suggests; so Big Daddy is sick, though he won't accept it. As Williams notes, the point is not "one man's psychological problem," but "a common crisis."[16]

The half-heard character of homosexuality in discreet discourse has been theorized recently, in terms afforded by D.A. Miller, as an *open secret*. "In some sense," Miller observes, the secret is always open: its function "is not to conceal knowledge, so much as to conceal the knowledge of the knowledge."[17] It helps to constitute the public/private boundary—the binary that seems to demarcate our subjectivities from a public realm, while actually producing those subjectivities—and thus facilitates the policing of that boundary. The secret keeps a topic like homosexuality in the private sphere, but under surveillance, allowing it to hover on the edge of public visibility. If it gets fully into the open, it attains public recognition; yet it must not disappear altogether, for then it would be beyond control and would no longer effect a general surveillance of aberrant desire. The open secret constitutes homosexuality as the "unthinkable" alternative—so awful that it can be envisaged only as private, yet always obscurely available as a public penalty for deviance.

Miller is working with the new historicist interpretation of Foucault —preoccupied with the entrapment model, whereby even subversion contributes to containment. In nineteenth-century novels Miller observes "the attempt of the protagonist to break away from the social control that thereby reclaims him" (p. 27); I discussed this in the previous chapter, and how cultural materialists try to theorize a space for dissidence. Miller's title, *The Novel and the Police*, suggests the repressive state apparatus, but he finds that social order is accomplished mainly through ideological self-policing—through "various technologies of the self and its sexuality, which administer the subject's own contribution to the intensive and continuous 'pastoral' care that liberal society proposes to take of each and every one of its charges." Policing, Miller says, moves "out of the streets, as it were, into the closet—I mean, into the private and domestic sphere on which the very identity of the liberal subject depends" (pp. viii–ix).

Identifying privacy and self-policing with the closet is richly suggestive—as in Eve Sedgwick's deployment of the idea in *Epistemology of the Closet*. However, insofar as such self-policing is being identified as the principal mode through which surveillance is exercised in societies like ours—as a general effect inherent in the whole modern concept of subjectivity, registering "the subject's accommodation to a totalizing system that has obliterated the difference he would make"[18]; insofar as the open secret is doing all that, merging it with homosexual oppression may obscure distinctions in the historic opportunities for lesbians and gay men. Exploring the diverse historical conditions in which notions of same-sex passion have circulated is a good way of defending ourselves against them.

The texts called literary, like other texts, disclose a range of maneuvers in relation to homosexuality. At one extreme, D.H. Lawrence wrote an opening chapter to *Women in Love* in which Birkin's erotic feelings for men are detailed, and then deleted it. There are numerous instances of such specific censorship. Also, there are less direct kinds of censorship—re-sexing the pronouns (to use a phrase of Auden's)—by Proust, notoriously. At the other extreme, we have texts from cultures where the boundaries of sexuality were drawn so differently—for instance in Shakespeare's time, I argued in chapter one—that it is difficult to discern a viable equivalence with our own patterns. In between, there are authors whose presentation of male eroticism is certainly interesting to us, but to whom we still cannot confidently attribute a modern gay awareness. The explicitness of such texts is often surprising: if they knew what we know, surely they couldn't have written it like that. I'm thinking of Tennyson and Melville; Whitman and Hopkins, perhaps.

It is a fundamental analytic mistake to suppose that, in these obscure cases, authors really had a concept of gayness like our own, but placed a mask over it; that it is lurking, therefore, behind the text—as if it were a statue under a sheet, entirely there but waiting to be revealed. To suppose this would be an unhistorical use of the Machereyan ideological silence. And even where we have reason to believe the author re-sexed the pronouns, it cannot be adequate simply to "translate" the text back into a supposed original. As David Savran puts it, "recklessly transposing both gender and sexuality" produces "an unintelligible clutter whose only coherence becomes the ill-concealed homosexuality of its author."[19]

To be sure, there is good reason for students of sexualities to dwell on self-policing and entrapment: subordinate groups are vulnerable to self-oppression—internalizing demeaning images of oneself. What is so appalling about Cold War U.S. notions of sexuality is that gay people believed them. Tennessee Williams applied to himself the familiar story of failed manhood. At the age of eight he was kept in bed for a year by diphtheria: "During this period of illness and solitary games, my mother's overly solicitous attention planted in me the makings of a sissy, much to my father's discontent. I was becoming a decided hybrid, different from the family line of frontiersmen-heroes of east Tennessee." His unsympathetic father, on the other hand, had grown up "mostly without the emollient influence of a mother." In the late 1950s Williams submitted himself to analysis. His "strict Freudian" urged him "to attempt a heterosexual life" and to give up his lover of ten years standing, Frank Merlo. The relationship did break up, for various reasons, and Merlo died. Williams wrote: "As long as Frank was well, I was happy. He had a gift for creating life and, when he ceased to be alive, I couldn't create a life for myself. So I went into a seven-year depression."[20] The analyst's attempt to destroy the relationship was based on a stupid and prejudiced theory.

The open secret is not used simply in the Cold War ideological milieu of *Cat on a Hot Tin Roof*. For Skipper the effect was fatal; for Brick it is fraught; for Big Daddy it is not a problem, and scarcely for Maggie; other characters seem virtually unaware of it. Furthermore, the situation is not static: the play moves towards openness, and the characters handle this in diverse ways. Maggie and Big Daddy are talking about homosexuality plainly enough; they both say, in fact, that secrecy is blocking Brick's career and relationships. The play is not secretive; it is about secrecy, and about how people would be happier if they lived differently.

In other societies elsewhere and hitherto, same-sex passion has been a secret but not open; or open and not a secret; or inconceivable altogether. The situation of women and men has usually been different. The U.K. parliament was so discreet about lesbianism in 1921 that it wouldn't even legislate against it; to do so might "bring it to the notice of women who have never heard of it, never thought of it, never dreamt of it," said the Director of Public Prosecutions.[21] This entire range, in respect of openness, pertains in our societies today, in varying circumstances. Not recognizing this may lead to an assumption that lesbians and gay men are trapped eternally by their sexuality as such (this might be a psychoanalytic perspective), and hence discourage political action. In the rallying cry, Silence = Death, we assert that secrecy about the concerns of gay men makes their early and painful deaths more likely; openness makes a difference.

Dissident Strategies

David Savran, in his important account of Williams, argues that the plays are revolutionary in their rejection of domestic realism: they undermine "the hegemonic and hierarchical structure of masculinity itself by disclosing the contradictions on which its normative formulation is based." They do this primarily, Savran says, through "a process of *desubjectification*, an unbinding and deconstruction of the sovereign subject"; through "a profligacy of words that disrupts traditional notions of narrative continuity and dramatic forms."[22]

A quest for the "right" artistic form dominated Marxist literary theory in mid-century, when Brecht disputed with Lukacs as to whether "realism" required a recognizable presentation of social reality or an analytic slant upon it; the topic was revisited by Althusserians in the 1970s (as I remark in chapter two).[23] Savran relates the constructedness of gender to the Brechtian principle that dramatic form should expose the constructedness of ideology. If the most powerful strategy of ideology is making its dispositions appear natural, the theory runs, then the project of a dissident theatre must be to *de*naturalize by disrupting any prospect of stable stage illusion. Arthur Miller has often been regarded as the radical dramatist of the 1950s, but his "dramaturgy remains strictly teleological, moving towards a future that has already happened, a peripety that is always a disclosure of the past," Savran says (p. 31). The structure of Williams's plays, conversely, "is adamantly plural, strewn with multivalent symbols, and reluctant to provide the interpreter with a master perspective or code" (p. 98). Savran compares *Cat on a Hot Tin Roof* with Brecht's *The Good Person of Szechwan*: "the action of the play cannot be disentangled until those watching or reading it resolve the material contradictions that structure the culture in which they live" (p. 102).

The problem with this formulation, as Savran recognizes, is the general critical acclaim with which Williams's best-known plays have been received. Of course, most of these critics do not take Williams as a Brechtian writer (that would make him even more un-American). One move is to shift the plays into a reactionary, tragic, "absurdist," or post-tragic framework. For Benjamin Nelson they are about "the loneliness of human existence"; for Roger Boxill, Williams is "an elegiac writer, a poet of nostalgia."[24] This is the antithesis of radical commitment. Another move is to celebrate Williams as flawed and dangerous, but nonetheless a great, tormented, "American" playwright. In fact, to be tormentedly *un*-American was, in one sense, to affirm America—first as a site where profound, "universal" passions might be enacted, and second as the implicit healthy norm for the majority who do not aspire to tragic stature. Marion Magid, in an essay of 1963, remarks the strange image a European would have of the United States if Williams's plays were the only source. Yet Williams is

American after all—"in his passion for absolutes, in his longing for purity, in his absence of ideas, in the extreme discomfort with which he inhabits his own body and soul, in his apocalyptic view of sex."[25] Well, the U.S. people I know are not much like that. To get her great American dramatist, Magid is easing Williams into a plausible America, adjusting the one to match the other. Sacvan Bercovitch presents this kind of maneuver as typical: "all our classic writers (to varying degrees) labored against the [American] myth as well as within it. All of them felt, privately at least, as oppressed by Americanism as liberated by it. And all of them, however captivated by the national dream, also *used* the dream to reach beyond the categories of their culture."[26] It is part of the myth of "America" that it renews itself through confrontations with itself. So Williams's dissidence is part of his American genius—part of *the* American genius—and nothing need be done about anything.

It is not sufficient to regard complacent interpreters as insensitive to Williams's true revolutionary potential; they indicate the ways his texts have actually circulated. It is a key proposition in cultural materialism that the historical conditions in which cultural institutions and formations organize and are organized by textualities must be addressed. Further, the truly dissident dramatic (or literary) form—Brechtian or otherwise—is, in my view, a chimera.

In developing his argument about Williams's disruptive potential, Savran draws upon the work of theorists of lesbian performance art, such as Kate Davy, Sue-Ellen Case, Jill Dolan and Teresa de Lauretis. Davy praises the way Split Britches' production of Holly Hughes's text, *Dress Suits to Hire* (1987), denaturalized conventional ideas of gender and sexuality by disrupting any prospect of stable stage illusion. "The operations of theatrical representation are over-determined, foregrounded, and made visible, thereby undermining, paradoxically, the construction of *woman as body*." The performance "scrambles the signals, the processes of identification."[27] And apparently it worked—for a heterosexual, though avant-garde, audience. However, when *Dress Suits* was presented at the University of Michigan, "in a conventional theatre setting, in the legitimate (and legitimizing) institutional setting of a major university, the work's potential to subvert dominant ideology was seriously undermined," Davy says (p. 166). Sue-Ellen Case, who had admired Split Britches' *Beauty and the Beast*, also thought this: she saw the audience at *Dress Suits* being gleefully entertained.[28]

Lynda Hart reappraises the principle of theater strategy by considering

Split Britches' *Anniversary Waltz*, as performed at the University of Pennsylvania in 1990. Despite dramatic techniques which, in Hart's view, "upset expectations of conventional narrativity, linearity, or causality," a broadly progressive audience largely ignored the lesbian theme. "Numerous spectators commented on the familiar themes and wide-based appeal of the performance"; there was "an almost seamless repudiation of any lesbian presence." What was probably happening there, as Hart suggests, is a well-meaning, liberal attempt to assimilate lesbians as "just like everyone else"—which, of course, is incompatible with the project of subverting the sex-gender system.[29]

When Hughes presented *Sins of Omission/Snatches*, at the Institute of Contemporary Arts in London in September 1993, there was nothing disjunctive in the latter part of her performance: she spoke to us as if delivering a personal message. An audience mainly of lesbians was delighted with some shrewd revisiting of traditional topics, but disconcerted, I thought, to hear finally that the problem is "our shame." They may well have been supposing that the problem is that when you behave without shame you may risk getting fired or beaten up or arrested. The stress on shame "did come as a surprise to me and I was uncomfortable with it being, as I remember it, the crunch-point, the dénouement," one woman tells me. "Maybe I am naive, or just lucky, but I do not feel shame in my daily life, nor do I think it is a particularly helpful way for lesbians to think." To be sure, it is crucial to address self-oppression, but in the context of hetero-patriarchal dominance, not as an apparent deep consequence of dissident sexuality. Hughes appeared locked in a negotiation with middle America; this would perhaps have spoken to some British lesbians, for it is indeed difficult to maintain pride in the face of persistent disconfirmation; but it was largely residual to an avant-gardist, metropolitan, audience. And what might heterosexual audience members make of it? They might deduce that they should try not to make lesbians feel so bad; equally, they might infer that lesbians are doomed to be either deeply shameful or brazenly shameless. This instance, also, illustrates how political impact depends upon audience and institutional setting.

In her article "Sexual Indifference and Lesbian Representation," Teresa de Lauretis assesses many diverse modes through which "lesbian writers and artists have sought variously to escape gender, to deny it, transcend it, or perform it in excess, and to inscribe the erotic in cryptic, allegorical, realistic, camp, or other modes of representation."[30] All of these are worth trying; there is no magical answer. The mistake is to expect a single stylistic maneuver to have a reliable effect—either dissident or conformist. Dollimore observes: "Nothing can be intrinsically or essentially subversive in the sense that prior to the event subversiveness can be more than potential; in other words it cannot be guaranteed a priori, independent of articulation, context and reception."[31] The task is not to specify the one, true strategy, but to be flexible and cunning—as the dominant is.

Traditional Englit invokes "the audience" as a unitary, unproblematic category whose "responses" may be inferred from the text; this allows the critic to proceed blithely with an unsituated "reading," thereby effacing the possibility of readers from subordinated groups. In practice, the one performance may be (for instance) reinforcing for lesbian-identified women and disconcerting for others. Class and educational background also matter. As Lukacs complained, Brechtian techniques may be regarded as avant-gardist or elitist (they may be the modes of music hall, but that is not how they are being used; they feature to reactionary purposes in high modernism). Some audiences are more ready to handle stylistic disjunctions than others. I return to some of these questions in the next chapter.

Containment Strategies

"So how do you know when you're being dissident?" Anne Middleton asked in a seminar at Berkeley: When they come at dawn, take you away, and lock you up. Cultural dissidence is not usually treated that seriously in our societies, but there are other ways of inhibiting its impact. *Cat on a Hot Tin Roof* was a scandalous success because it addressed the disturbed but necessary question of latency. But part of the cultural work provoked in that success—the condition under which the text circulated—was the nervous restoration of the secrecy that Williams had violated. As D.A. Miller puts it, "the fact the secret is always known—and, in some obscure sense, known to be known—never interferes with the incessant activity of keeping it." This was happening when Brooks Atkinson reviewed the initial (1955) production without mentioning Brick's relationship with Skipper. Walter Kerr, in the *New York Herald Tribune*, acknowledged "the implication" of "an unnatural relationship" but complained that *Cat* exhibits "a tantalizing reluctance" to "blurt out its promised secret."[32] In fact, the play is plain enough; Kerr needs there to be a secret. A standard tabloid story in the U.K. is the shock-discovery of the gayness of someone who has not in fact been hiding it. The need is to insist that it is the kind of thing anyone would conceal if they could.

Attempts to contain *Cat* began with Elia Kazan, the first director of the play. He thought Brick should "undergo some apparent mutation" as a result of the exposure of his anxieties. Hence the change in the stage directions at the end, whereby Brick seems to incline towards renewing sexual relations with Maggie. So even if Brick is latently queer, he may be sorted out through therapeutic experiences and the devotion of an understanding woman. Williams was unhappy at this change—he did not "believe that a conversation, however revelatory, ever effects so immediate change in the heart or even conduct of a person in Brick's state of spiritual disrepair."[33] This is, of course, right: if the problem derives from "a common crisis" in the prevailing family and social structure, it won't be solved by interpersonal maneuvering, even on a more sustained basis than occurs here. Williams was trying to refuse a central tenet of bourgeois literary culture—that people gain significant individual autonomy through personal experience.

The further changes that were required to make *Cat* into an acceptable movie, in 1958, closed off the secret of queerness almost entirely. The project, said the director Richard Brooks, was "writing the homosexuality out of Brick's character." So the script stressed "Brick's basic immaturity, his refusal to grow up and meet the responsibilities of adult life." This might be enough, Brooks thought, to motivate Brick's rejection of "manhood as understood by Big Daddy, by a sensual wife, by most of middleclass America."[34] Skipper, even, had to be exculpated. In the play, Maggie says she and he wanted to sleep together to get closer to Brick, but Skipper couldn't make it with her (pp. 55–56, 59). In the film, Maggie tries to seduce Skip because she is jealous that the boys pay so much attention to football (!), and Skip is manfully enthusiastic; but Maggie draws back in case she loses Brick. In the film, Brick's underlying heterosexuality is indicated when he is shown burying his face in Maggie's slip and caressing it in agony. And in the introductory scene with Maggie, he is made to "wield his crutch in a series of phallic positions" that suggest, to one commentator at least, "that he has a sexual disability, rather than a deviance."[35] Trivial as this may sound, it was the key to the project: Brick's limb is fractured temporarily, and sensitive treatment should work a cure (this, of course, was the psychoanalysts' line on homosexuality, and the one preferred by Kazan).

Even so, *Cat* could not quite be fitted back into the closet. A key psychoanalytic notion was that homosexuality is related to immaturity, so the film's dependence on that only partly blurred the issue. Also, some movie-goers knew what the play had been about. So the suggestion remained in the film for those who felt able to see it. One reviewer thought it "played down the deviation motif"; another declared Brick "the best dramatized study of homosexuality I have seen."[36] Such indeterminacy is of course characteristic of the operation of the open secret.

By the late 1950s, partly through the work of people such as Williams, partly because homosexuality was being invoked continually as the awful other that had to be disavowed, the secret was opening, and hence became a topic of discreet, and malicious, allusion. In 1958, Robert Brustein attacked William Inge as "the first spokesman for a matriarchal America." The theme of Inge's plays, Brustein says, was the emasculation of the male; he was following Williams "in writing she-dramas, in giving to women if not the leading role then certainly the pivotal (and most insightfully created) role in his work." As if featuring women were not bad enough, Inge and Williams had introduced a dubious kind of hero: the "male impersonator," who wears blue jeans, cowboy boots and tee-shirt and is credited with athletic prowess, but "hides fundamental insecurities behind an exaggerated show of maleness."[37] Symonds's Adonis, perhaps. Stanley Kauffmann took up the topic in 1966, now with Edward Albee in mind, as well as Williams and Inge. Their attitudes toward family values are un-American: "Because three of the most successful American playwrights of the last twenty years are (reputed) homosexuals and because their plays often treat of women and marriage, therefore, it is said, postwar American drama presents a badly distorted picture of American women, marriage, and society in general." This happens because gays are bitter and twisted: "there is every reason to expect their plays to be streaked with vindictiveness toward the society that constructs and, theatrically, discriminates against them."[38] The reversal is quite precise. Williams and Albee say the recommended version of heterosexual relations is corrupt and corrupting; hostile critics reverse the charge, alleging that gays don't like American values because, being un-American, they can't join in.

Kauffmann asks: "If there are heterosexuals who have talent equivalent with those three men, why aren't these 'normal' people writing? Why don't they counterbalance or correct the distorted picture?" (p. 292). The inference is that it has been a mistake to entrust Americanness to gay writers. They may be allowed to produce culture—to produce America—

but only on condition that they efface themselves and maintain an overt respect for patriarchy.

As with Shakespeare's work, deciding whether Williams's plays are, in essence, progressive or reactionary is in my view not a viable project. They have held the stage before basically conservative, boulevard audiences. At the same time, successful plays are usually risky; they flirt, at least, with the danger that prevailing values might not be satisfactory, or might not prevail. Sexuality is an unstable construct in our societies, and hence produces endless textual work. Such an awkward issue has continually to be revisited, disavowed, rediscovered, reaffirmed. Closure, by definition, is always potentially unsatisfactory; even conservative texts are often to be found pushing representation to a breaking point where contradiction cannot plausibly be contained. In the face of such a performance, some audience members will retreat into conformity, while others will entertain more radical possibilities. These texts were, and are, sites of struggle; and their varying re-presentations *are* that struggle.

Sexual Citizenship

Despite the official embargo, innumerable people in the U.S. military are, in fact, reckoned by those around them to be gay—this is repeatedly attested in interviews conducted by Steven Zeeland near a U.S. base at Frankfurt. Allan Bérubé comments: "While a few have been targeted for discharge or were the victims of antigay violence, most portray a social milieu of sexually-tense tolerance." In particular, it is assumed that certain jobs are typically done by homosexuals—signal corpsmen, cooks, medics, and clerks.[39] So the military accommodates gay men up to a point, and in so doing exploits them to reinforce its dominant masculine ethos by cultivating a masculine/feminine split within its personnel.

I suspect that the current positioning of sexual deviance, as a spectrum extending from relatively "good" types at one end (monogamous, same-age couples who keep their homes nice without drawing attention to themselves or aspiring to rear children) to "bad" types at the other (child-molesters and the like), suits the prevailing ideological conjuncture very well. It gives politicians, the media, religious leaders, and their ilk ample to chew on. The relative invisibility of lesbians, for instance, allows the notion that women are not "like that" (they don't assert themselves and can't manage without men), while leaving sufficient space for demonizing those who insist on indicating otherwise.[40]

It is not so much that rights achieved so far by lesbians and gay men are contested; but that our societies seem well able to live with that contest. Numerous particular gains may be made, and many of us are so inured to our situation as to be almost pathetically grateful for them. But, overall, we have reached a structural point from which it is going to be hard to advance very far. The difficulty, I believe, is not incidental or circumstantial. The increased visibility of lesbians and gay men over the last twenty-five years has transformed our opportunities; at the same time, it has made us more accessible to hostile appropriation. Before gay liberation, many people report having supposed themselves to be the only one. Now the secret is more open and we are besieged with representations of ourselves, but few of these are such as we would choose. The trick, today, is to have us here BUT disgraceful.

In an important recent study, *Sexual Citizenship*, David T. Evans shows how our societies have positioned same-sex potential, holding it at a systematic distance from the rights of citizenship. Those rights have often been categorized as civil (individual liberty, freedom of speech and association, property, justice), political (opportunities to influence government) and social (the area addressed by welfare provision). Plainly lesbians and gay men are discriminated against in all these areas. This, Evans shows, is made to appear proper through a new distinction made in the Report of the Wolfenden Committee on Homosexual Offences and Prostitution (1957): between morality and legality.[41] Homosexual practices are located in a private realm where, though immoral, they may not require the attention of the law. So Wolfenden wanted to retain penalties for public soliciting, and it is in fact unlawful in the U.K. to propose to someone a sexual act that is, in itself, lawful. Despite the legalizing of many gay sexual practices in private, the alleged immorality of lesbians and gay men seems to justify the withholding of full citizenship in numerous, diverse respects—especially in familial and quasi-familial contexts, from parenting and fostering to schools and entertainment in the home (television). Indeed, the positing of a private space has made it seem appropriate to police the public sphere with special rigor. At the same time, the private space is far from secure. To the contrary, the public/private boundary has become an obsessive focus for legal maneuvering.

The ultimate question is this: Is homosexuality intolerable? If lesbians

are actually pretty much like other people, then it just needs a
is to come out, so that the anxious among our compatriots
't really so dreadful, and then everyone will live and let live;
...ty will become unimportant. But if homosexuality does undermine
orthodox constructs of masculinity, femininity, and the family, and those
constructs are indeed fundamental to our present kind of society, then
lesbians and gay men may well constitute a profound challenge to so-called
American or western values. And the tabloid newspapers and TV evangel-
ists may have good reason to be hostile.

Since, in my view, these matters are constituted culturally, they are in
principle accessible to political intervention. However, the disappointments of the postwar years, such as I was discussing in the previous
chapter, show how hard it can be to shift deeply embedded social formations. "As long as society is based on competitiveness and sexual repression," Denis Altman observes, "there will be a need to demarcate it
into categories, to maintain socially induced repressions by stigmatizing
heavily all those who fall outside the norm."[42] In Hans Mayer's view,
discrimination against outsiders is endemic to our societies; it manifests
the historic failure of Enlightenment principles. The eighteenth-century
ideal of equality was abandoned at the point where the bourgeoisie gained
control and founded its order "only on economic inequality, albeit within
the framework of a universal equality so far as the letter of the law is
concerned. This order transformed women into parasitic slaves since they
did not earn money and were not supposed to. It fought Jewish emanci-
pation via education and property. It was xenophobic from the start and
became increasingly nationalistic. . . . From now on there would be the
normal and the degenerate, worthwhile and worthless human life."[43] This
was written in 1975; in the time of HIV and AIDS it screams off the page.
Our societies proclaim an ideology of equal opportunity, but they operate
by producing and stigmatizing a whole range of outsiders.

Once we envisioned a relaxed sexual regime in which any of us might
do almost anything. But sexual indeterminacy is truly distressing to very
many people—because it acts, in Sedgwick's phrasing, as "an unpredicta-
bly powerful solvent of stable identities."[44] People have been socialized
into sexualities and general attitudes that suit, or once suited, the maintenance of our kind of social system, and they don't want their identities
dispersed. Like some animals reared in captivity, they don't want to be
"liberated." Furthermore, progressive social attitudes seem to correlate, in
our societies, with economic well-being. Under the current pressures of

urban collapse, worldwide economic slump and ecologica'
want to hang on to what they think they've got.

Yet the prevailing structures produce us, as well as
literally true—unlike ethnic groups, lesbians and gay men arc ⹁
straight community that harasses them. The compulsory nuclear fan⹁
and the stigmatization of same-sex passion are related to the urban anomie
that accompanies capitalism; but so are the weakening of the family and
gay liberation. Within such broad structural faultlines, innumerable local
contradictions flourish. The Section 28 law forbade U.K. municipalities to
spend money in ways that might promote homosexuality; it was designed
to inhibit the circulation of lesbian and gay cultures and, by causing municipalities to withdraw from certain projects, it has done that. However, it
also brought out onto the streets a generation that had become complacent with its discos and decor. And lesbians and gay men recognized a
common cause virtually for the first time; this was a precise response to
Parliament, for the first time, legislating against women and men together.
Even the U.S. military, despite its antigay policy, functions as an opportunity for young men, and I daresay women, to "find themselves"
homosexually—enabling them to escape their small-town and family envi-
ronment and experience a foreign city such as Frankfurt.[45]

Whether lesbians and gay men will prove intolerable, or not, and
whether sexualities generally will be liberated or closed down, is going to
depend on the balance of forces. The point of principle is the one I was
proposing in relation to dissidence and entrapment in the previous chapter: the outcome will depend on what we all do in the historical conjuncture. There is a good deal still to play for.

4. Beyond Englit

The Truest Poetry

In his poem "The Truest Poetry is the Most Feigning," published in 1955, W.H. Auden urges upon love poets the most elaborate style: "Be subtle, various, ornamental, clever. . . . From such ingenious fibs are poems born." This is the best way to court "your Beatrice," and it may help you in times of political violence:

> If half-way through such praises of your dear,
> Riot and shooting fill the streets with fear,
> And overnight as in some terror dream
> Poets are suspect with the New Regime,
> Stick at your desk and hold your panic in,
> What you are writing may still save your skin:
> Re-sex the pronouns, add a few details,
> And, lo, a panegyric ode which hails
> (How is the Censor, bless his heart, to know?)
> The new pot-bellied Generalissimo.[1]

"Re-sex the pronouns," "such ingenious fibs": forgive me if I seem obsessed, but this sounds like a closeted gay aesthetic. Hostility from the authorities in affairs of the heart is not experienced only by lesbians and gay men, but the topic does bite with a certain shrewdness for them. The joke in the poem is that to please the vain dictator you change your pronouns *to* the same sex.

I wrote about this in my book, *Literature, Politics and Culture in Postwar Britain*, and my treatment has been challenged by my old friend Laurence Lerner, in an article in *New Literary History*. His thesis is that some ways of reading would better be described as "unwriting"—he specifies literary biography, ideological criticism, and textual scholarship. He prefers a criticism "marked by its respect for the process of writing and its wish to preserve the integrity of the result."[2] To Lerner, "The Truest Poetry is the Most Feigning" is about how "a love poem derives its value from the writing, not from what it tells us about love." In his view, this is not an ideological proposition; it is the cultural materialist who introduces that kind of thing. "To the cultural materialist," Lerner says, "there has to be an agenda behind this, and Sinfield claims to have sniffed it out." Like all too many critics today, I am not "reading" but "decoding" in a "structuralist" manner. Instead, we should "read Auden's poems for the meaning they offer," and then "we shall have no reason to see any homosexuality in them" (pp. 801–3).

Englit, traditionally, never has had "reason to see any homosexuality." In 1944 Robert Duncan's poem "An African Elegy" had been accepted by John Crowe Ransom for the *Kenyon Review*. But then Duncan's essay "The Homosexual in Society" was published—a bold though quite modest proposal. In Ransom's view, the essay changed the meaning of the poem. Now it seemed to have "obvious homosexual advertisement, and for that reason not to be eligible for publication." Ransom asked: "Is it not possible you have made the sexual inferences inescapable, and the poem unavailable?" What had been impressive in a shadowy way now had to be read as of gay significance, and hence no longer passed as poetry—i.e., as heterosexual. The story was similar with *Partisan Review, Hudson Review, Southern Review, Sewanee Review*.[3] In 1967 M.L. Rosenthal, in his book *The New Poets*, discussed Duncan as "probably the figure with the richest natural genius among the Black Mountain poets." However, "In a number of the poems . . . an acceptance of homosexual love is taken for granted; that is, it is assumed that everyone will share the poet's felt meanings."[4] In the ordinary way of things, most critics would say that the invitation to share unaccustomed "felt meanings" is a special pleasure of poetry. We don't live in Cumberland, but we become fuller people by sharing Wordsworth's experience. But gay experience is different—there are some feats of imagination the Englit reader can't be expected to attempt. Rosenthal concludes: "there is little question that even the sympathetic and sensitive reader of poetry will find it hard to come to sympathetic terms with everything that Duncan writes" (pp. 183–84). The possibility of gay readers is not entertained; "the sympathetic and sensitive reader of poetry" is heterosexual by definition. Don't imagine such attitudes are quaint. The 1986 Picador edition of Edmund White's *Caracole* declares on the fly-leaf: "Until now he has been best known for his books about the gay experience, especially the non fiction *States of Desire: Travels in Gay America* and the novels *A Boy's Own Story* and *Nocturnes for the King of Naples*. But with *Caracole* he devotes himself to an examination of a larger world."

We should "read Auden's poems for the meaning they offer," Lerner says. But to whom is this "meaning" "offered"? Evidently it is offered to him. More broadly, I extrapolate, it is offered to two overlapping reading formations: the poetry-reading public, and Englit. This overlap is the reading position Lerner occupies. For him, inside those formations, they don't need justifying; he is simply reading the poem. Such taking-for-granted is understandable, for already, by the time Auden was writing "The Truest Poetry," the poetry-reading public and Englit formations existed in modes very like their current ones. If the poem had been written earlier, or in another place, Lerner's reading position would be more obviously problematic; but in an instance such as this, it is not unreasonable to suppose that W.H. Auden anticipated just such readers as Laurence Lerner. Even so, this *is* a specific reading position, as we can see if we remind ourselves that it is one not readily available to the majority of people in our cultures (who are not at ease with poetry-reading or Englit). Suppose my historic socialization and current social insertion are different from Lerner's, such that I do not altogether occupy his reading position, share his reading formation?—in fact it is evident in my book that I am reading partly as a gay man.

Lerner's answer is that gay critics should read and write as if they were someone else. "Suspension of disbelief and scholarly responsibility would make one a kind of provisional . . . heterosexual as one reads," he suggests.[5] That is the historic stance of Englit. It is what the Harvard critic F.O. Matthieson did in his book *American Renaissance*—Matthieson was perhaps the gay equivalent of Lionel Trilling. He wrote, about Walt Whitman, of "the passivity of the poet's body," finding there "a quality vaguely pathological and homosexual" (and Shelley comes off badly once more). To be sure, Matthieson adds, Whitman "did not simply exhibit pathological symptoms; he created poetry." But the problem with that formulation is that it defines poetry as that which is not homosexual. Matthiessen wrote quite differently about Whitman to his lover.[6]

A gay reading position was available, like Lerner's, in something like its current form in 1955, when "The Truest Poetry" was published: there was a gay subculture recognizably continuous with our own, and Auden's homosexuality was known to some and widely rumored to others. Lerner allows that there will have been gay readers: "That Auden was a homosexual is well known, and it is perfectly possible, even likely, that some of his friends winked when they read his love poems and gave an extra smirk" (they don't sound very attractive). "But in doing this they were not reading the poems; they were noticing a rag of extraneous meaning that had got stuck onto them—or onto some copies of them, the copies his friends read. They, like Sinfield, were unwriting them."[7] Lerner recognizes a minority readership, people in the know, but disallows them—even though, as Auden's "friends," their interpretation might be thought quite authoritative. Of course, these "friends" by and large did not publish their reading; they were inhibited by the very pressures that I think Auden was writing about in the poem. Gay reading is thus triply inhibited: Auden writes indirectly about indirection, and those in the know handle that indirectly.

In my reading of "The Truest poetry," Auden's point is that poetic indirection is not insincere because readers know the score:

> Though honest Iagos, true to form will write
> *Shame!* in your margins, *Toady! Hypocrite!*
> True hearts, clear heads will hear the note of glory
> And put inverted commas round the story,
> Thinking—*Old Sly-boots! We shall never know*
> *Her name or nature. Well, it's better so.*

"True hearts" will "put inverted commas round the story"; they will know how to read indirectly. The phrase "Old Sly-boots" was used by Auden as the title for a review of J.R. Ackerley's book *My Father and Myself* (1960), in which Ackerley describes how he discovered evidence of his father's homosexuality. Similarly, the poem uses the phrase "tall tales," which is almost "tall story," a phrase Auden uses in an essay on Cavafy (1961), where he praises Cavafy's boldness on the subject of homosexuality but then defends discretion. "In the arts, one must distinguish, of course, between the lie and the tall story that the audience is not expected to believe," he says.[8]

Gay men are quite likely to find themselves involved in Audenesque indirections because they have always been associated with the poetry-reading public and Englit—so long as we are discreet, that is. Indeed, it is often asserted that gay discretion is beneficial to literary culture. Ransom thought homosexuals such as Duncan should "sublimate their problem, let the delicacy and subtlety of their sensibility come out in the innocent regions of life and literature."[9] This means that a good number of already-prestigious texts may engage our concern. This relationship with the mainstream is different for different subordinated groups. People of color may find little there; Jews don't need *The Merchant of Venice*. For feminists it may be just a matter of reversal (instead of celebrating the marriages in

Twelfth Night, you may deplore them); at the same time, there are a great many hitherto-suppressed texts by women. Lesbians, currently, are asserting a tradition of popular culture, from romance writers of the 1950s and 1960s, such as Ann Bannon and Valerie Taylor, to more recent romance, thriller, and science fiction writing.[10] But gay men seem doomed to wrestle with the canon. A further consequence is that few of our historical texts actually affirm our sexualities. Oscar Wilde's celebrated speech about the love that dare not speak its name—when you come to look at it—is justifying non-sexual love. "My image of Oscar in the dock loses its halo," Neil Bartlett observes; "He lied, and he lied at a crucial moment in our history, just when we were about to appear. If he had 'told the truth,' everything might have been different."[11]

So it is a matter, in part at least, of finding a culture in the margins of the dominant. I have suggested in an article on Noel Coward that some of his plays anticipate two audiences: a knowing and a naive one; one that picked up gay references, and one that didn't.[12] We may regard this as a guerilla campaign wherein gay men courageously and inventively sustained a private subculture under the noses of the censor; that is how "The Truest Poetry" invites us to see it. Alternatively, we may regard it as a cop-out. During those decades, homosexuality was denied the status of public utterance while being sufficiently present, nevertheless, to effect a surveillance of dissident sexualities. For homosexuality was censored, not absent. Compare Edmund Spenser's poem *The Shepheardes Calender*: scholarship discovers there covert criticism of the Elizabethan government. But who was supposed to understand such criticism? If no one, then what was the point? Actually, of course some people must have understood, otherwise we couldn't now reconstruct those covert inferences; so the government did get criticized. But why allow covert, but not overt, criticism? The answer is that dissidence is least threatening when it can be seen to be respecting boundaries. Annabel Patterson argues that in early-modern England there evolved, quite consciously, "a joint project, a cultural bargain between writers and political leaders." There were "conventions that both sides accepted as to how far a writer could go in explicit address to the contentious issues of his day, how he could encode his opinions so that nobody would be *required* to make an example of him."[13] That is like the open secret, which I discussed in the previous chapter: manifest discretion protects the dominant by indicating that boundaries are respected.

The issue, still, is how to break this pattern. For gay discretion helps to shield Englit from the implications of an effeminacy which (I argued in chapter two) it cannot altogether avoid. Gay men, consequently, have not had a bad time in Englit and literary culture—provided, of course, that they can tolerate the humiliation of passing; as Adrienne Rich puts it, "Be more like us and you can be almost one of us."[14] A further corollary has been the relative exclusion of women—hiring them seemed at once superfluous (a sensitive man might understand everything relevant to the writing of Jane Austen) and scandalous (if women do it well it might not be a manly occupation).

Lately it has become fairly easy to have a lesbian or gay personal life in an Englit department—though it is safer not to be too explicit until you've got the job. I remember, with affection, Larry Lerner asking, perhaps in 1972, if my partner and I would like a pot of his home-made jam. That was all right, wasn't it?—he was signaling that he regarded us as a legitimate domestic set-up. The harder question, still, is whether gayness may be permitted to intrude upon Englit; serving his jam at a gay tea party is one thing, but elbowing in on his poem is another.

Subcultures

Janice Radway's study, *Reading the Romance*, suggests how reading formations relate to subcultures. "There are patterns or regularities to what viewers and readers bring to texts and media messages[,] in large part because they acquire specific cultural competencies as a result of their particular social location. Similar readings are produced, I argue, because similarly located readers learn a similar set of reading strategies and interpretive codes which they bring to bear upon the texts they encounter."[15] From this perspective, we can theorize the security guard of my first chapter who was able, in defiance of dominant endorsement of the bard, to hate *The Merchant of Venice*: he felt authorized by his Jewish subculture. In similar vein, we can theorize the situation of Englit: it too is a subcultural formation. Lerner says that while there are indeed "particular reading communities or subcultures . . . there is a central reading from which such particulars diverge, which we call the meaning of the poem."[16] "We," in that sentence, means people socialized into Englit, which Lerner defines as "central"; I regard it as another, rather arrogant, subculture. It is not, I argued in chapter two, dominant in our societies—the dominant is located, surely, in the military-industrial complex and the financial, class and political establishment, and is coded masculine. Nonetheless, Englit is strong, and thoroughly adapted to its allocated roles.

And we can theorize the scope for lesbian and gay subcultures. Teresa de Lauretis quotes Elizabeth Ellsworth's findings in respect of the film *Personal Best* (1982): lesbian feminist reviewers adjusted the meanings proposed in conventional (Hollywood) codes of representation. They redefined the protagonist, ignored sections focused on heterosexual romance, disregarded the actual ending, and discovered apparently unintended erotic moments. Such contest over interpretation, Ellsworth argues, "is a constitutive process for marginal subjectivities, as well as an important form of resistance." "Dykonstruction," Sally Munt calls it in her introduction to *New Lesbian Criticism*.[17] Barbara Bradby, considering how lesbians cultivate a mythic status for popular music performers, links such appropriation to Foucault's argument that the author *function* is a mode of perception that gets attached to some writing: "In this sense, the invention of the mythic or fantasy identity of the popular performer is what serves as the social basis for the circulation of certain discourses in popular music as lesbian discourses." Apprehending these performers through a subcultural framework contributes to "the ongoing process of constructing lesbian identities in everyday life."[18]

The dominant ideology tends to constitute subjectivities that will find "natural" its view of the world (hence its dominance); this happens in subcultures also, but in ways that may validate dissident subjectivities. In that bit of the world where the subculture runs you may feel confident, as we used to say, that Black is beautiful, gay is good. There, those stories work, they build their own kinds of interactive plausibility. "In acquiring one's conception of the world one belongs to a particular grouping which is that of all the social elements which share the same mode of thinking and acting," Antonio Gramsci observes.[19] It is through such sharing—through interaction with others who are engaged with compatible preoccupations—that one may develop a plausible alternative subject position. To be sure, everyone is constructed by the dominant ideology through, we may say, the state apparatuses. But ideology, Althusser stresses, is lived in day-to-day interactions, and these socialize us also into subcultures of class, ethnicity, gender and sexuality, which may be in some respects oppositional; or at least negotiated.

These two terms—oppositional and negotiated—indicate two ways of handling the dominant that groups are likely to use. They were proposed by Frank Parkin, and taken up by Raymond Williams and Stuart Hall, principally as a way of theorizing a relation to the mass media other than the passive reception often imagined in Frankfurt School work.[20] Three major decoding systems may be discovered in our kinds of society: the dominant, the negotiated, and the radical or oppositional. The dominant deploys the framework of understandings that successfully claims normative status; members of subordinated groups may subscribe to it through fear, deference, or aspiration. Negotiated systems adapt the dominant system or accommodate to it, rather than endorse or oppose it. This, I would say, is how many people handle the day-to-day requirement that they acquiesce in a social structure that affords them little dignity or satisfaction. Englit is, by and large, a negotiated formation. A radical decoding system sustains an oppositional stance toward the dominant; such systems have been articulated, historically, through the politically aware sectors of various groupings, drawing upon class, ethnic, gender and sexual allegiances. Subcultures must not be invested, romantically, with the potential magically to see through, or resist, capitalism and patriarchy, but they do hold a potential for dissidence. In her book *The Currency of Eros*, Ann Rosalind Jones shows how the dominant-negotiated-oppositional framework makes sense of sixteenth-century women writers.[21]

To be sure, there are problems in applying subcultural theory. Its initial British users were blind to gender, as was quickly pointed out.[22] Tania Modleski denies the appropriateness of subculture in gender studies, arguing, in relation to Radway's study,

> that the interpretive conventions enabling us to read romances are not formed in a community or subculture like the one studied by Radway but are, for *most* of us, set in place from birth, that in a patriarchal society a female child is born into and simultaneously interpellated by a world where many of the conventions of romance hold powerful sway—in, say, her mother's fantasy life (which in turn shapes her own life at the level of the unconscious), in popular songs and fairy tales, and later, in novels and movies. These conventions are, then, part of our cultural heritage as women.[23]

This is right, but rather than an argument against subcultures, it is a good analysis of how they get constituted. "The cultural heritage of women" may be regarded as a subcultural formation, deriving from socialization processes comparable to those that constitute ethnic subcultures.

The obvious question that arises with putting it that way is whether it is reasonable to consider half the population as a subculture. On the one hand, that might seem to push women, dismissively, to the margins of the social process. On the other hand, it might seem to suppress the differences among women (many would dispute Modleski's suggestion that all women have the same reading formation in relation to romance). Even in the face of these dangers, however, we do need a model for theorizing ways of viewing the world that seem particular to women, without supposing subjectivist or essentialist notions, such as personal intuition or biological woman-ness. The advantage of subculture as an interpretive tool is that it designates a distinctive framework of under-standing that is neither determined by the dominant nor miraculously immune to it. It suggests how non-dominant attitudes get transmitted, and how subcultures become adept at handling the dominant while retain-ing some independence from it.

In my view, whether all women—or members of any subordinated group—belong to diverse subcultures, or to one, is not a matter of prin-ciple, but an operational question—dependent on the kind of cultural analysis or political alignment one is attempting. For some purposes it might be better to distinguish older and younger women, lesbian and straight women, Black and white women; for others, not. For some pur-poses, it might be relevant to look at the ways in which Black women and Black men share the same formation. These are, after all, the demarcations that people use when they think about themselves. Subcultures should not be envisaged as homogeneous or as having clearly defined boundaries. Most of us have some part in several, and how this should be handled depends on the analytic focus that seems desirable in a given instance. Looking back on *Reading the Romance*, Radway feels she was too narrowly preoccupied with gender, and would now want to study other variables— "age, class location, education and race."[24] And, one might add, sexuality.

De Lauretis warns against "the presumption of a unified lesbian viewer/reader, gifted with undivided and non-contradictory subjectivity." As a Black lesbian in the 1950s, Audre Lorde experienced these issues urgently and complexly. Lorde's white lover "seemed to believe that as lesbians, we were all outsiders and all equal in our outsiderhood. 'We're all niggers,' she used to say."[25] To Lorde it was not all the same.

For some of us there was no particular place, and we grabbed whatever we could from wherever we found space, comfort, quiet, a smile, non-judgment. *Being women together was not enough. We were different. Being gay-girls together was not enough. We were different. Being Black together was not enough. We were*

different. Being Black women together was not enough. We were different. Being
Black dykes together was not enough. We were different. Each of us had our own
needs and pursuits, and many different alliances. (p. 226)

Subcultural alignments are never sufficient, Lorde says (there are individuals), but for dissident identity they are always necessary. The weakness of
Black lesbian subculture was the big problem. "It was hard enough to be
Black, to be Black and female, to be Black, female, and gay. To be Black,
female, gay, and out of the closet . . . was considered by many Black
lesbians to be simply suicidal" (p. 224). Despairing of the United States
after the executions of Ethel and Julius Rosenberg, who were alleged to
have shared atom secrets with the Soviets (and to have had a marriage in
which the woman was the stronger partner), Lorde traveled to Mexico,
where she found "brown faces of every hue meeting mine." It was "an
affirmation for me that was brand-new and very exciting. I had never felt
visible before, nor even known I lacked it" (p. 156). Being surrounded by
people of color allowed Lorde to see herself in ways that white domination
had not. Yet lesbianism remained invisible, since the progressive expatriots
with whom she mainly associated concealed their sexuality (p. 160). Subculture is crucial to self-perception.

The boundaries of lesbian and gay subcultures are distinctively confused. As Sedgwick has observed, there are two ways of thinking about
sexuality. One is *universalizing*: it supposes that innumerable people have a
homosexual component in their make-up. The other is *minoritizing*: it
supposes "that there is a distinct population of persons who 'really are'
gay."[26] Western cultures tend, incoherently, to credit both models. In the
1950s, the universalizing model of latency was invoked alongside the minoritizing idea that gays might be an identifiable subversive malfunction
that may be weeded out. "I believe that there have always been Black dykes
around—in the sense of powerful and women-oriented women—who
would rather have died than use that name for themselves. And that includes my momma," Lorde declares. But elsewhere in *Zami* she shows her
mother's antipathy to her daughter's lesbian lifestyle, and recalls "how
being young and Black and gay and lonely felt. . . . There were no
mothers, no sisters, no heroes." It is utopian fantasy when she imagines
how "the mothers and fathers smiled at us in greeting as we strolled down
to Eighth Avenue, hand in hand."[27]

Both models have dissident potential. The universalizing concept of a
"lesbian continuum" enables Adrienne Rich to call upon women generally

to de-prioritize relations falling inside the oppressive pattern that currently informs heterosexuality, and to build powerful interactions with other women.[28] The minoritizing model may help us to identify and consolidate our constituency, and to draw convenient analogues with racial minorities. Conversely, there is security in neither model. If everyone is potentially gay, anxiety about expressing that gayness and consequent hostility might be the greater. If few of us really are, it might be easier to scapegoat us.

It is the same with the question of whether homosexuality is acquired or innate. If acquired, lesbians and gay men can boldly assert our choices; on the other hand, we may be judged to have perversely chosen a wrong or inferior lifestyle. If we are genetically determined, it might seem futile to harass people who are only manifesting a natural condition; on the other hand, our enemies might regard us as an inferior species, an affront to an alleged evolutionary or religious demand that sex be in the service of procreation. Simon LeVay, a gay scientist who believes he has located a part of the brain that is distinctively formed in gay men, hopes this will allow recognition of lesbians and gays as a minority whose characteristics are immutable, and hence civil rights protection from the U.S. Supreme Court (so we can benefit like the American Indians). The drawback is illustrated in an exchange between LeVay and his father—who is entirely persuaded by his son's work. So how does LeVay senior see gay men now? He says he regards Simon as he would a child born with spina bifida, a hare lip, or some other developmental defect. LeVay junior finds this "pretty humiliating"—though I don't see why he should, since it is a logical consequence of his theory. Indeed, the attraction of stigmatization is depressingly apparent; people with spina bifida may well feel their civil rights are violated when they are appropriated as the awful other by LeVay, senior and junior.[29] LeVay is not alone in his genetic project. Researchers at the U.S. National Cancer Institute claim to have located "a genetic factor" in homosexuality. It seems you should be on the look out for gay uncles and cousins on your mother's side (work on lesbians, as usual, has not been so ardently pursued). In Britain, the item was picked up from the journal *Science* as the front page lead in the *Independent* newspaper, and television and radio news carried the item through the day.[30] The talk was all of whether people would wish to abort potentially gay offspring.

The flaw in these genetic studies is not the laboratory method, about which I am not qualified to comment, but the assumption of a unitary "gay man" as the already-known object of analysis. "The category 'gay' is not, and has never been, merely a personal label-like category, implying some kind of essence," Simon Watney observes. Rather, "gay" asserts "a political and legal *unity of interests* between subjects variously categorised as perverse/sick/mad/queer/contagious and so on."[31] Not all people who engage in same-sex practices regard themselves as gay or homosexual, or are so regarded by others; and not all people who regard themselves as gay or homosexual, or are regarded as such by others, engage in same-sex practices. As Jeffrey Weeks observes, someone we might regard as "a homosexual prostitute" may not identify himself or herself either as a homosexual or as a prostitute.[32] In the National Cancer Institute study, 76 homosexual men were investigated, and it was found that more of their brothers were gay than would be expected in the general population. The flaw should be obvious here: people who are ready to acknowledge their own gayness are vastly more likely (a) to realize, and (b) to admit, that they have gay siblings! It is all to do with perceptions and identifications.

"It is pointless to investigate the root causes of homosexuality," Diana Fuss says, if we realize that it is "not a transhistorical, transcultural, eternal category but a socially contingent and variant construction."[33] The case on whether homosexuality is genetic or acquired, or whether it is the property of a minority or of everyone, can be made either way—*because* it all depends on what is meant by homosexuality! The initial decision about the "it" that is to be investigated shapes the outcome. If we say "it" is the occurrence of any same-sex act, or of any intense same-sex bonding, then we will find hardly anyone to be immune and arrive at a universalizing model. If we require an acknowledged identity or engagement in a gay lifestyle before accepting that "real" homosexuality is present, we will find fewer instances and hence arrive at a minoritizing model. Gayness is not, primarily or interestingly, a property of individuals, but a mode of categorizing that circulates in societies like ours. It is a principal way that we use to demarcate the range of sexual potential. Trying to decide who the real homosexuals are, therefore, is to join the ideological circus, not to gain a vantage upon it.

Actually, there are very many ways of experiencing same-sex passion —as there are cross-sex passion; many people manifest several of them, together and at different points in time. One advantage in the National Cancer Institute study, Robert Pool believes, writing in the journal *Science*, is that it won't be subject to falling apart in the way that happened when genetic determination of manic depression was claimed: in the latter case, people from the "wrong" side of the sample developed previously unsuspected symptoms.[34] This is a very odd notion; in fact very many people move between gay and heterosexual relationships. To display the range of experience, Sue George in her book *Women and Bisexuality* uses the Klein Sexual Orientation Grid, whereby you have to say on a scale of one to seven, in respect of past, present, and ideal, whether you are more straight or gay in respect of seven aspects: sexual attraction, sexual behavior, fantasies, emotional preference, social preference, self-identification, lifestyle. This gives thousands of possible variants.[35]

Our terms—"gay," "lesbian," "lesbian and gay," "lesbian, gay and bisexual," "dyke," "queer"—are markers of political allegiance, far more than ways of having or thinking about sex. We are encouraged to envisage these terms as identifying specific forms of desire and practice, but immensely diverse behaviors and fantasies find some place within them. They represent decisions about who we want to be aligned with, carved out in ongoing negotiations with the available repertoire. This can be complex. "Sexually I am bisexual with a strong lesbian identity; politically I identify as gay/lesbian," one woman writes.[36]

Hence the intermittent and, I hope, careful place of lesbianism in the present study: lesbians and gay men have different histories. I have written inclusively wherever that has seemed plausible, but I am proposing thereby a political alignment, not that we are "the same." Some women, whom I respect, will regard such an alignment as inappropriate, or at least premature. That is for them to say—on some issues, plainly, we have different interests, and a gay man is still a man. In my view, all groups should be as separate as they want, and should talk to adjacent groups if, when, and as much as they want.

Beyond Englit

In fact, Englit can accommodate my reading of "The Truest Poetry." It might be seen as a helpful one, responding to a subtext as well as to the apparent meaning, and the poem might be praised for a special range and subtlety of implication.

Lee Edelman, mindful of the way "our critical institutions" define the concerns of gay men and lesbians as "narrowly specialized (ie. insignificant)," encourages us to envisage "ways in which a gay reading practice that attends to the social inscriptions of ideology can make visible certain definitive stresses inhabiting our culture's texts."[37] So lesbian and gay reading would help everyone sharpen up their critique. This is we. lesbian and gay readings that hunt the queer without attending to the whole sex/gender system are bound to be inadequate, and literary critics who want to concern themselves with culture will certainly discover crucial faultlines around homosexuality. However, that is not the move I wish to encourage today. I do not want, as the highest priority, the incorporation of lesbian and gay reading into Englit. I want something both less and more ambitious. It is right for us to deploy the expertises that have been developed in and around humanities departments, but we need to think also about how we are going to take them back to the lives of lesbians and gay men. I want to assert that Auden's writing belongs to male gay subculture, and always did, as well as to Englit. And that members of gay subculture will and should do with Auden as they wish (if others find our deliberations interesting, that's all right).

Literary criticism, says Stanley Fish, is like a game with rules; it is a "disciplinary performance" that "depends on the in-place force of innumerable and enabling connections and affiliations."[38] This can be oppressive. Ed Cohen has written of what it took to get him and gay work into *PMLA* and Rutgers (I note also, thinking back to my initial discussion of *The Merchant of Venice*, that Cohen describes himself as Jewish, academic and gay; but only the latter two get considered).[39] Hazel Carby has regretted the way Black feminist criticism "for the main part accepts the prevailing paradigms predominant in the academy, as has women's studies and Afro-American studies, and seeks to organize itself as a discipline in the same way"; Barbara Ehrenreich makes a similar point.[40] It has been depressing to watch North American lesbian and gay studies getting incorporated into the academic star system, which requires that an individual who makes a notable contribution be hugely feted and rewarded, so that in the ensuing phase everyone else can feel justified in gathering round and attacking him or her, thereby furthering their own careers. This is perhaps easier to say from the U.K., where lesbian and gay studies is unthinkable outside a general left-wing orientation; and hence is accompanied by a serious suspicion of the market, cultural hierarchy, and the education system as an ideological state apparatus or bank of cultural capital; and hence of Englit. We feel uneasy at institutional success, and love that Walter Benjamin quote about there being "no document of civilization which is not at the same time a document of barbarism."[41] Anyway, we don't have the money to sustain a star system.

The more ground lesbian and gay studies gains in Englit, the more the gulf widens with other lesbians and gay men—with gay men particularly, since they have often found the person of letters tradition important and rewarding. Art is one of the places where gay men have secured some respect from straight culture. Richard Dyer has written about how he experienced this as a teenager. "Queerness brought with it artistic sensitivity—it gave you the capacity to appreciate and respond to culture. It was a compensation for having been born or made queer. . . . It also made you doubly 'different'—queer and cultured. And how splendid to be different! Even if you were awful."[42] In this tradition, style, taste and sensibility are still active criteria, and academic aspirations towards intellectual rigor seem unsympathetic and inappropriate. In recent years, Thomas Piontek has remarked, there has been a "burgeoning of gay literature," but "one would not know this from looking at academic publications."[43]

Actually, Fish's "game" analogy is misleading, because we can stretch, violate and extend the rules of the academy; there will be a cost, but we can do it. Fish denies that one can achieve a "performance self-consciously larger than its institutional situation would seem to allow" (entrapment again). But then, realizing, I suppose, that he is being silly, Fish adds a note: if one did "adopt such a focus," then one "would no longer be doing literary criticism."[44] Well, that is the point, the price: we can develop wider intellectual vistas, but we might "no longer be doing literary criticism." I am proposing a shift in self-conceptualization, away from the category: Englit professionals engaged in lesbian and/or gay studies, towards the category: lesbian and/or gay intellectuals.

For intellectuals are important: they help to maintain or undermine belief in the legitimacy of the prevailing power arrangements. They help to set the boundaries of the thinkable. They confirm or rework the stories through which we tell each other who we are. Gramsci is a good reference point because he acknowledges that all people are intellectual and endorses a wisdom in common sense, while also specifying as a social category the people who perform the social function of intellectuals. Gramsci distinguishes organic and traditional intellectuals: the former are organic to their class, whereas the latter, who in his society were mostly gentlemen of means, "put themselves forward as autonomous and independent of the dominant social group." One way of making political ground is to capture the traditional intellectuals, but "ideally," Gramsci says, "the proletariat should be able to generate its own 'organic' intellectuals within the class who remain intellectuals *of* their class."[45] Of course, academics can turn out on a political demonstration, like other people. I am demanding something more specific: that the lesbian and gay movements generate organic intellectuals.

To be sure, there are problems with this idea. The overwhelming proportion of intellectuals today, Foucault points out, are in professional and managerial occupations. They are employed—usually to exercise particular skills, often by big business or the state. Traditional intellectuals spoke as arbiters of truth and justice, as expounders of universal truths; professional intellectuals exercise their effect through the particular terms and circumstances of their work.[46] This account is specially illuminating in relation to Englit, where the initial claim to speak for Man—out of what was, in practice, largely a class confidence—has slithered into mere professional expertise. (It is for this that we are expected to desert our subcultures of family and neighbourhood, of class and ethnicity.) It has become difficult to work as an intellectual at all, Foucault indicates, without becoming enmeshed in occupational patterns—in one of Fish's games. In fact, Edward Said observes, the word "intellectual" is often displaced in the U.S.A. by "words like 'professional' and 'scholar' and 'academic'," and this correlates with "the general refusal of American Left intellectuals to accept their political role."[47] At this point a resuscitation of the idea of organic intellectuals makes sense.

It will not be a matter of voluntaristic personal decision, or just of writing different kinds of academic papers; but of discovering further institutional opportunities. Radway readily grants Angela McRobbie's point, that academic feminists tend to underestimate the potential of "ordinary" women and girls. And what they may need is "our support rather than our criticism or direction. To find a way to provide such support, however, . . . is not easy for we lack the space and channels for integrating our practices with theirs."[48] We have to find those channels. Cornel West calls for Black intellectuals to seek roots in "the broader institutions in civil society, whatever they are and in whatever role— the trade unions, the mass media as a cultural worker, or in musical production or video production, or a preacher, or what have you."[49] bell hooks believes it can be done: "It's not like I'm going to talk about writing and thinking about postmodernism with other academics and/or intellectuals and not discuss these ideas with underclass non-academic black folks who are family, friends, and comrades. . . . critics, writers, and academics have to give the same critical attention to nurturing and cultivating our ties to black people that we give to writing articles, teaching, and lecturing."[50]

Applying the terms I introduced earlier, this may produce an oppositional rather than a negotiated relation with Englit.

This is not to say that we should become exclusive; rather, it is because exclusivity is impossible—because Englit is so powerful, and because gayness is so inextricably involved with heterosexuality—that this priority needs asserting. Certainly I am not arguing against finding common causes with other groups; I do believe, though, that we have to get our base right first. Gay men have to get themselves better sorted out before they can expect other groups to take them very seriously. I am not even arguing against infiltrating Englit; I do lesbian and gay studies myself, and agree strongly with Piontek that there is no one, privileged site of gay activism.[51] I am proposing a priority: that we try to stop thinking of lesbian and gay studies as a sufficient objective. Ask not what we can do for Englit, but whether it can do anything for lesbian and gay people.

As Carby has shown with respect to the Harlem Renaissance and other Black movements in the early part of the century, intellectuals have to be wary of presuming to define and speak for a people.[52] It is not a matter of knowing best, or of establishing a correct line, but of trying to use our hard-won skills to illuminate histories and problems. There are problems enough in our relations with straight society, and, at least as importantly, among ourselves—misogyny, racism, bisexuality, sado-masochism, self-oppression, class and inter-generational differences, HIV and AIDS. I realize that the idea of subcultural intellectuals sounds pretentious, but it's better than getting sucked into professional Englit—hiding in universities, using long words, and getting to be big fish in a small pond.

The Largest Gathering of the Decade

The ultimate question is how far contributing to the dominant is likely to protect any subordinated group. I've had this argument with Thom Gunn, in an interview and in correspondence. Is he a gay poet, or a poet who is gay? "At times," he says, "I do think of myself as writing for a gay audience." He has written poems for publication in the gay press in San Francisco, where he lives. However, Gunn adds: "I don't usually think very precisely about the matter of audience; I doubt if many writers do, unless they are deliberately writing for a specialized audience, like writing boys' adventure novels." My reply is: if you don't think about your audience, in practice you fall into the customary voice of poetry. "Don't you just end up writing for the normal Faber and Faber poetry audience?," I ask Gunn—writing, in effect, for Lerner's Englit and poetry-reading formations.[53]

I want to end by talking about Gunn's book of poems, *The Man with Night Sweats*. Many of the poems are about gay love; roughly a third are about AIDS. In "Courtesies of the Interregnum," Gunn tells how a friend, who once had hosted weekly gatherings, is now pleased to report that he is able to eat hot food at all. The friend becomes aware that his illness is excluding the poet—not a person with AIDS—who is still his guest:

> He is, confronted by a guest so fit,
> Almost concerned lest I feel out of it,
> Excluded from the invitation list
> To the largest gathering of the decade, missed
> From membership as if the club were full.[54]

The civil intimacy of their relationship reasserts itself, maintaining the fitness of guest and host after all. Through "such informal courtesy" the host, an athlete, achieves a triumph—"with not physical but social strength." In the face of AIDS, gay community is more, not less, necessary and rewarding. What is supporting both Gunn and his friend is "social strength," their shared subcultural experience, both now and in a continuity with the past.

The virulence of the hostility toward gay men that the AIDS pandemic has released, it occurs to me, is proportionate to the idea, which was getting into general circulation around 1980, that gays were doing better with the sex-and-love questions. We seemed to have learned a few tricks that straights had yet to develop. Gay men had organized genial ways of meeting for casual sex, and also loving couples that might manage, even, to evade gendered roles. They knew how to see other men without falling out with their partners; how to go to bed with friends, how to remain on close terms with former lovers, how to handle age and class differences. They were at ease experimenting with kinky games; they were getting the fun back into sex. For the right-wing bigot, therefore, AIDS was a godsend. It countermanded, precisely, that alleged gay advantage. It had all been a fantasy—"the family" should set the limits of human experience. For Camille Paglia, AIDS is the price of sexual adventure. "We asked: why should I obey this law? and why shouldn't I act on every sexual impulse? The result was a descent into barbarism. We painfully discovered that a just society cannot, in fact, function if everyone does his own thing. And out of the pagan promiscuity of the Sixties came AIDS." Like the markets, you can't buck nature. Hence, according to Paglia, the death of Foucault: he "was struck down by the elemental force he repressed and edited out of his system."[55]

The importance of Gunn's poems is that they reassert the initial vision. The fact that we have run into AIDS does not mean the vision was wrong—any more than hemophiliacs were wrong to have blood transfusions (though Paglia's logic would mean they were trying to countermand nature, and should just have gone on and died in the first place). In "The Missing," Gunn celebrates not just his friends, many of whom have died, but a continuing vision of love which depends on distinctive and recognizable assumptions of gay culture:

> Contact of friend led to another friend,
> Supple entwinement through the living mass
> Which for all that I knew might have no end,
> Image of an unlimited embrace. (p. 80)

Now many of these friends are dying, but their loss does not show that the project of an unlimited embrace was wrong; it shows just how right it was and how much it is needed now. "Memory Unsettled" records a comforting in a hospital bed that alludes to the idea of a renewed sexual encounter:

> You climbed in there beside him
> And hugged him plain in view,
> Though you were sick enough,
> And had your own fears too. (p. 76)

The new right says AIDS shows that such a vision of sexual community is wrong; the poem says that AIDS makes gay civil intimacy more, not less, necessary and rewarding.

I want to say that this vision is not just a theme in these poems: it is the enabling condition of them. For writing about AIDS is difficult. How to match the scale of the thing, how to avoid appearing to use it? Gunn's poems work, I believe, because the deaths they record are not only a personal concern—and not merely a "universal" one either. They are points of subcultural engagement. In San Francisco, there are organizations for people who test HIV *negative*—to enable them to contribute, to feel less guilty at being "fit." When I met Gunn there, in 1989, the *Bay Area Reporter*, a give-away paper, had a dozen and more obituaries each week. Perhaps two hundred words; just who they were, how old, what they did, what they were like, how their lover and friends and (often) relatives miss them; a small photo. But, unlike other obituaries, these are all the same: all AIDS deaths. For that "largest gathering of the decade," in Gunn's phrase, there is a public significance to dying. Most of us have expected that our ceasing-to-be will be of note only to friends and family in the ordinary sequence of life. But this dying is part of a huge, continuing, subcultural event—civil and yet intimate. These poems are part of that. And this, I think, is what enables Gunn to write them, and what makes them valuable.

Gunn writes to me that he believes he is using, in the main, a voice that is not universal or "human," and not specifically gay either; just his own. Thus he shows that "being gay is as normal as anything else; so when I write about my life as a gay man, or with a gay emphasis, I am implicitly saying that I don't have to put on a special voice to speak about such matters." I reply that this is still a version of the Faber voice. However, I have to admit that Gunn's deployment of that voice may indeed, despite my main argument, be oppositional. For, to be sure, subcultures cannot evade involvement with the dominant—often they are positioned as its defining others. As Michael Bronski observes, a subculture "creates and recreates itself—politically and artistically—along with, as well as in reaction to, the prevailing cultural norms. No counterculture can define itself independently of the dominant culture."[56] Through this very involvement, subcultures may return from the margins to trouble the center. They may redeploy its most cherished values, abusing, downgrading, or inverting them; willy-nilly, they exploit its incoherences and contradictions. So they form points from which repression may become apparent, its silences audible. In a brilliant passage in *Operation Shylock*, Philip Roth points out that Irving Berlin, a Jew, wrote "Easter Parade" and "White Christmas": "The two holidays that celebrate the divinity of Christ—the divinity that's the very heart of the Jewish rejection of Christianity . . . Easter he turns into a fashion show and Christmas into a holiday about snow. Gone is the gore and the murder of Christ—down with the crucifix and up with the bonnet! *He turns their religion into schlock.* But nicely! Nicely! So nicely the goyim don't even know what hit 'em."[57]

Gunn's poems may be doing something like this. *The Man with Night Sweats* has a good deal to say about family. The first poem in the book, "The Hug," finds the poet and his domestic partner of thirty years and more in bed together after a party. They hug:

> It was not sex, but I could feel
> The whole strength of your body set,
>   Or braced, to mine,
>   And locking me to you
> As if we were still twenty-two
> When our grand passion had not yet
>   Become familial. (p. 3)

In "The Missing," Gunn writes of his friends, many of whom have died, as "an involved increasing family" (p. 80). The volume ends with "A Blank", in which Gunn catches sight of an erstwhile lover who has adopted a child. This could be the corniest humanist closure, could it not?—thou mettest with things dying, I with things new born. But, of course, the politics are far more challenging. For the qualities that the poet's friend is devoting to the child are continuous with those he developed as a gay lover:

>   he transposed
> The expectations he took out at dark
> —Of Eros playing, features undisclosed—
> Into another pitch, where he might work
> With the same melody, and opted so
> To educate, permit, guide, feed, keep warm,
> And love a child. (pp. 84–85)

And this is not, they tell us, how families are supposed to be formed.

Now, this is a provocative move—consider the U.K. Section 28 law, which prevents municipalities from spending money to suggest that gays may have "pretended families," or the book, *The Anita Bryant Story: The Survival of Our Nation's Families and the Threat of Militant Homosexuality*. It is also a risky move—our understanding of the scope for new kinds of personal relations may be inhibited by perceiving them through older, largely hostile formations. Anna Wilson argues that Lorde's reinvestment in "mothers and fathers" in *Zami* suggests "a crucial lack of alternative conceptualizations through which to imagine community. . . . Traditions are not, after all, families." Lorde's "final repositioning within an accepting community depends," Wilson shows, "not on a rediscovery of Black lesbian origins but on a reimagination of them."[58] The value of invoking mainstream structures depends, surely, on whether one is seeking to appropriate their legitimacy or reveal their limitations. Gunn may well hope that the specificity of the San Francisco subculture in his poems will demand a radical reading—that his re-use of family will effect what Jonathan Dollimore calls "transgressive reinscription": "the subculture, even as it imitates, reproducing itself in terms of its exclusion, also demystifies, producing a knowledge of the dominant which excludes it."[59]

However, the mainstream has the advantage of virtually endless recuperative maneuvers. Apart from my review in the *London Review of Books*, only one U.K. treatment of *The Man with Night Sweats* mentions family: Gunn in the *Independent on Sunday* draws it to the attention of an interviewer who doesn't follow it up. Faber kindly sent me ten reviews from English papers, one Scots and one Irish. Only the *Western Morning News* admits to being disturbed, warning that "some people will probably be offended" and that the volume "may not be welcome by all." Elsewhere the pronouns are not re-sexed—Gunn's text hardly permits that—but not one reviewer takes the evident viewpoint of a gay man. Rather, they subtly countermand Gunn's emphasis on the continuing validity of gay subcultural modes. One notices "how a time of hard-won freedoms, of limitless potential and hedonistic release, has turned into a time of plague" (*Independent on Sunday*); another congratulates Gunn on setting limits to "the candour of out-of-the-closet sexual freedom" (*Weekend Telegraph*).[60] The commonest tactic is to discuss poetic technique; repeatedly, gay experiences in the poems are exonerated (as it is presented) on the ground that they have produced literature. So the *Observer* consoles itself with the thought of "art's heroism as well as its uselessness," and the *Independent* concludes that "there is no disaster so complete that it cannot refresh a poet's art." That there might be something ghoolish in such welcoming of poetic life at the expense of human death seems not to be registered. The *Economist's* reviewer recalls being unimpressed by Gunn's volume *Passages of Joy* (1982), because it "deals with homosexuality happily"; now Gunn has learned better, and AIDS "has given his poetry more life and more raw human vigour than it has ever had before."[61] The only good gay is a dead gay.

Members of subordinated groups are prone to assume that subcultural work is all very well, but the mainstream is what counts. This is self-oppressed. To be sure, get Faber to publish your poems if you can; without such institutions I'd have difficulty reaching you with these thoughts. But mainstream recognition is by mainstream criteria. When Jeanette Winterson's novel *Oranges Are Not the Only Fruit* was adapted for BBC television in 1990, with explicit lesbian love-making, Winterson believed it challenged "the virtues of the home, the power of the church and the supposed normality of heterosexuality." Cherry Smyth, a queer critic, wrote in *Spare Rib* of "a breakthrough for a mainstream TV drama slot," praising a "refreshing lack of embarrassment and shame" in the sex scenes. In some newspapers the idea of lesbian sexuality was mocked, but Winterson was pleased when the series was "overwhelmingly well received." However, as Hilary Hinds has shown, mainstream critics accomplished this by presenting *Oranges* as "about" everything other than lesbianism. It was "a vengeful satire on Protestant fundamentalism" (*The Listener*); "a wonderfully witty, bitter-sweet celebration of the miracle that more children do not murder their parents" (*Observer*); "fundamentally about a young person looking for love" (*Today*). The *Todmordern News* said *Oranges* "follows Jess in a voyage of self-discovery from her intense religious background, via a friendship with another girl."[62]

The center takes what it wants, and under pressure will abuse and abandon the subcultures it has plundered. Black and Jewish people, it seems to me, have reason to know this. While AIDS was thought to affect only gay men, governments did almost nothing about it; but for gay subculture, thousands more would be dying now. Subordinated groups gain more self-respect, more community feeling, and a better self-understanding by insisting on their own explicit subculture—history, fiction, music, cultural commentary. If, as Benjamin said, there is "no document of civilization which is not at the same time a document of barbarism," the contributor from a subordinated group may experience a special complicity and sorrow. If he or she "writes a masterpiece," Jean Genet observes in his introduction to writing by the Black activist, George Jackson, it is the "enemy's treasury which is enriched by the additional jewel he [or she] has so furiously and lovingly carved."[63]

Mind you, art can be useful. It helped one respondent in *Between the Acts*, a collection of personal histories recounted by elderly gay men. Norman was born in 1895; by the time he was in his late twenties he had not knowingly met a homosexual—so closed was the secret to most people at that time. Things happened between men, but "they all saw it as something different." Nonetheless, Norman did have fun: "When I was cuddling him he said, I let you do this, because you are an artist."[64]

Notes

Notes to Foreword

1. William Bennett, "To Reclaim a Legacy," 14–15.
2. E.D. Hirsch, Jr., *Cultural Literacy*, 92.
3. The *Times*, April 23, 1991.
4. Department of Education and Science, *English*, Key Stage 3, Tier 5–7 (London: Department of Education and Science, 1993), 16.
5. Adrienne Rich, *Blood, Bread and Poetry*, 199.
6. Kate Davy, "From *Lady Dick* to Ladylike: the Work of Holly Hughes," 78. See also Gabriele Griffin, *Heavenly Love?*, 187–88.

Notes to Chapter 1

1. John Gross, *Shylock*, 51; Lewis Simpson, *New York Times Book Review*, April 4, 1993, 7, 9.
2. Philip Roth, *Operation Shylock*, 274.
3. Lillian S. Robinson, *Sex, Class, and Culture*, 35. On Trilling, see Don Wayne, "Power, Politics, and the Shakespearean Text: Recent Criticism in England and the United States," 54–56; Alexander Bloom, *Prodigal Sons*, 142–44, 190–98
4. Adrienne Rich, "Split at the Root: An Essay on Jewish Identity," 227. See further James Yaffe, *The American Jews*; Russell Jacoby, *The Last Intellectuals*, ch. 4; Susanne Klingenstein, *Jews in the American Academy 1900–1940*.
5. Saguna Ramanathan, "Teaching English Literature in Post-colonial India"; Ania Loomba, *Gender, Race, Renaissance Drama*, 83–84. For a forceful account of the malleability of the Shakespearean text, see Terence Hawkes, *Meaning by Shakespeare*.
6. Lawrence Stone, *The Family, Sex and Marriage in England, 1500–1800*, 137.
7. Christopher Ricks, *T.S. Eliot and Prejudice*, 118.
8. Gross, *Shylock*, 127–63, 261–65.
9. David Thacker, "Understanding Shylock."
10. Arnold Wesker, *The Journalists/The Wedding Feast/Shylock*, 178.
11. Terry Eagleton, *William Shakespeare*, 37–38. Cf. Gross, *Shylock*, 318.
12. Allan Bloom with Harry V. Jaffa, *Shakespeare's Politics*, 21.
13. Bloom and Jaffa, *Shakespeare's Politics*, 28. See Allan Bloom, *The Closing of the American Mind*.

14. *Venus and Adonis*, lines 337–42, in Shakespeare, *The Poems*, ed. F.T. Prince.

15. Symonds, *The Memoirs of John Addington Symonds*, 62–63.

16. See W.H. Auden, "Brothers and Others," in *The Dyer's Hand*, 229–34; Hans Mayer, *Outsiders*, 279–82.

17. M.J. Wolff, *Shakespeare der Dichter und sein Werk*, 2 vols. I: 272–73, quoted in Shakespeare, *The Poems*, New Variorum Edition, ed. Hyder Edward Rollins, 505.

18. Douglas Bush, *Mythology and the Renaissance Tradition*, 146, quoted in *Poems*, ed. Rollins, 516.

19. C.L. Barber, *Shakespeare's Festive Comedy*, 244–45.

20. Coppélia Kahn, *Man's Estate*, 210–11.

21. See Laura Levine, "Men in Women's Clothing: Antitheatricality and Effeminization from 1579 to 1642"; Jean E. Howard, "Crossdressing, the Theatre and Gender Struggle in Early Modern England"; Stephen Orgel, "Nobody's Perfect: Or Why Did the English Stage Take Boys for Women?"; Jonathan Dollimore, *Sexual Dissidence*, ch. 19; Jonathan Goldberg, *Sodometries*, ch. 4.

22. Alan Sinfield, *Alfred Tennyson*, 128, also 17–21 and ch. 5.

23. Eric Partridge, *Shakespeare's Bawdy*, 13–18. Other critical evasions are amusingly displayed by Simon Shepherd, "Shakespeare's Private Drawer: Shakespeare and Homosexuality."

24. Garry O'Connor, *William Shakespeare a Life*, 95–96.

25. Michel Foucault, *The History of Sexuality*, vol. 1, *An Introduction*, 43.

26. Alan Bray, *Homosexuality in Renaissance England*, 16, 34, 88.

27. Bruce R. Smith, *Homosexual Desire in Shakespeare's England*, 13–14, 74–76. Cf. Alan Bray, "Homosexuality and the Signs of Male Friendship in Elizabethan England."

28. See Alan Sinfield, *Faultlines: Cultural Materialism and the Politics of Dissident Reading*, ch. 3.

29. Foucault, *History of Sexuality*, vol. 1, 43.

30. See Alan Sinfield, *The Wilde Century: Effeminacy, Oscar Wilde and the Queer Moment*.

31. *Samson Agonistes*, lines 410–11, in John Milton, *Poetical Works*.

32. Shakespeare, *Romeo and Juliet*, ed. Brian Gibbons, III.i.116.

33. Shakespeare, *Troilus and Cressida*, ed. Kenneth Palmer, V.i.13–16, III.iii.216–19.

34. Smith, *Homosexual Desire in Shakespeare's England*, 186, 197; and see 38–39, 59–66, 171.

35. David M. Halperin, *One Hundred Years of Homosexuality*, 25; Huseyin Tapinc, "Masculinity, Femininity and Turkish Male Homosexuality"; Stephen O. Murray, "The 'Underdevelopment' of Modern/Gay Homosexuality in Mesoamerica."

36. *Dido Queen of Carthage*, I.i.50–53, in *The Plays of Christopher Marlowe*, ed. Roma Gill. See Gregory Woods, "Body, Costume, and Desire in Christopher Marlowe"; Jonathan Goldberg, *Sodometries*, 126–37.

37. Shakespeare, *Antony and Cleopatra*, ed. M.R. Ridley, IV.i.1, II.v.22–23, III.xiii.17. See Janet Adelman, *Suffocating Mothers*, 184–92.

38. Shakespeare, *Coriolanus*, ed. Philip Brockbank, I.vi.29–32. For a comparable case with respect to *Henry V* and *Tamburlaine*, see Sinfield, *Faultlines*, 127–36, 237–38. See further Smith, *Homosexual Desire in Shakespeare's England*, ch. 2; David F. Greenberg, *The Construction of Homosexuality*, 333–35; Valerie Traub, *Desire and Anxiety*, 134–36.

39. Eve Kosofsky Sedgwick, *Between Men*, 25, 5, and 1–27 passim.

40. Bray, "Homosexuality and the Signs of Male Friendship," 14.

41. Goldberg, *Sodometries*, 20. See Traub, *Desire and Anxiety*, 105–13.

42. Traub, *Desire and Anxiety*, 93.

43. Bennett, "To Reclaim a Legacy," 15.

44. Goldberg, *Sodometries*, 11.

Notes to Chapter 2

1. Robert Paul Wolff, Barrington Moore, Jr., and Herbert Marcuse, *A Critique of Pure Tolerance*, 129, 98.

2. Louis Althusser, *Lenin and Philosophy and Other Essays*, 124.

3. Don E. Wayne, "New Historicism," 795. See further Jean E. Howard and Marion F. O'Connor, "Introduction"; Don E. Wayne, "Power, Politics, and the Shakespearean Text: Recent Criticism in England and the United States"; Walter Cohen, "Political Criticism of Shakespeare"; Louis Montrose, "Professing the Renaissance: The Poetics and Politics of Culture," 20–24; Alan Liu, "The Power of Formalism: The New Historicism."

4. Raymond Williams, *Problems in Materialism and Culture*, 35; Althusser, *Lenin and Philosophy*, 130.

5. Michel Foucault, *The History of Sexuality*, vol. 1, *An Introduction*, 95–96; Herbert Marcuse, *An Essay on Liberation*, 9.

6. Foucault, *History of Sexuality*, vol. 1, 96, 101. Cf. Ernesto Laclau and Chantal Mouffe, *Hegemony and Socialist Strategy*, 105–44

7. Fredric Jameson, *Marxism and Form*, 153–54.

8. Althusser, "A Letter on Art in Reply to André Daspre," in *Lenin and Philosophy*, 203–4.

9. Pierre Macherey, *A Theory of Literary Production*, 59–60.

10. Althusser, *Lenin and Philosophy*, 204.

11. Raymond Williams, *Culture and Society 1780–1950*, 307–8.

12. Raymond Williams, *Marxism and Literature*, 53, and 45–54; Pierre Macherey and Etienne Balibar, "Literature as an Ideological Form: Some Marxist Propositions." See also Raymond Williams, *Keywords*, 150–54; Tony Bennett, *Formalism and Marxism*; Terry Eagleton, *Literary Theory: An Introduction*.

13. Karl Marx, *Grundrisse*, 110–11. Cf. Terry Eagleton, *Marxism and Literary Criticism*, 10–13; Macherey, *Theory*, 70–71; Williams, *Marxism and Literature*, 52.

14. Elaine Showalter, "Toward a Feminist Poetics," 128.

15. Quoted by Margot Heinemann in Dollimore and Sinfield, eds., *Political Shakespeare*, 203. I argue in *Faultlines*, ch. 10, that bardic authority has been hijacked in distinctive ways in the United States.

16. Raymond Williams, *Culture*, 73–81.

17. Tennessee Williams, *The Theatre of Tennessee Williams*, vol. 4, 3–4.

18. Quoted in Ann Douglas, *The Feminization of American Culture*, 122.

19. Mary Poovey, *Uneven Developments*, 124; Boucherette is quoted by Poovey.

20. Virginia Woolf, *Three Guineas*, 103.

21. Charles Kingsley, *Literary and General Essays*, 43–44, 47, 51. I am grateful to David Alderson for drawing my attention to this essay.

22. Alfred Austin, "The Poetry of the Period," 120, 124.

23. Hume is quoted in Sandra M. Gilbert and Susan Gubar, *No Man's Land*, vol. 1: *The War of the Words*, 154.

24. Douglas, *The Feminization of American Culture*, 314.

25. Irving Babbitt, *Literature and the American College*, 118–19.

26. F.R. Leavis, *Revaluation*, 222, 221, 212.

27. Quoted in Leslie Fiedler, *Waiting for the End*, 263–64.

28. Fiedler, *Waiting for the End*, 223. See Donald Pease, "*Moby Dick* and the Cold War."

29. Havelock Ellis, *Sexual Inversion*, in Ellis, *Studies in the Psychology of Sex*, vol. 2, part 2, 57; see 51–56.

30. "Walt Whitman, Stranger," in Mark van Doren, *The Private Reader*, 71–73.

31. Kennedy is quoted by Fiedler, *Waiting for the End*, 273.

32. Allen Ginsberg, "America," in *"Howl" and Other Poems*, 34.

33. Macherey, *Theory*, 79.

34. See Alan Sinfield, *Faultlines*, 66–74, 95–108.

35. Nicos Poulantzas, *Political Power and Social Classes*, 207.

36. Ellis, *Sexual Inversion*, 291, 256. See also 110, 182, 190–91.

37. Symonds, *The Memoirs of John Addington Symonds*, 85; Shakespeare, *Antony and Cleopatra*, ed. M.R. Ridley, II.ii.214–16.

Notes to Chapter 3

1. Allan Bérubé, *Coming Out Under Fire*, 20.

2. Gustav Bychowski, "The Ego of Homosexuals," 125.

3. Audre Lorde, *Zami: A New Spelling of My Name*, 149. See John D'Emilio, *Making Trouble*, ch. 3; David Savran, *Communists, Cowboys, and Queers*, 1–29, 84–88.

4. See Sinfield, *Literature, Politics and Culture*, 109–12.

5. Kenneth Lewes, *The Psychoanalytic Theory of Male Homosexuality*, 168, quoting Abram Kardiner (1954); see Kardiner, "The Flight from Masculinity," 19, 38. See also Lee Edelman, "Tearooms and Sympathy, or, The Epistemology of the Water Closet."

6. Lionel Ovesey, "The Homosexual Conflict: an Adaptational Analysis." See Barbara Ehrenreich, *The Hearts of Men*, 24–25, and Lewes, *Psychoanalytic Theory*, 168.

7. Sigmund Freud, *Standard Edition of the Complete Psychological Works*, ed. James Strachey, vol. 23, 156.

8. Bérubé, *Coming Out*, 45–46, 143, 145–47.

9. Lewes, *Psychoanalytic Theory*, 136–37.

10. John M. Clum, *Acting Gay*, 15, and 11–16; see Savran, *Communists, Cowboys, and Queers*, 41–42.

11. Arthur Miller, *A View from the Bridge; All My Sons*, 66.

12. Norman Mailer, *Advertisements for Myself*, 193. See Dollimore, *Sexual Dissidence*, 46–47, 264–65; Georges-Michel Sarotte, *Like a Brother, Like a Lover*, ch. 19.

13. Irving Bieber, ed., *Homosexuality: A Psychoanalytic Study*, 14, also 10–11, 304; Lewes, *Psychoanalytic Theory*, 209, and ch. 6.

14. Tennessee Williams, *Cat on a Hot Tin Roof*, in *The Theatre of Tennessee Williams*, vol. 3, 57–58.

15. *Cat*, 121. Williams said probably this was all Brick and Skipper ever did, "and yet—his sexual nature was not innately 'normal' . . . . But Brick's overt sexual adjustment was, and must always remain, a heterosexual one": Maria St Just, ed., *Five O'Clock Angel*, 110. See Clum, *Acting Gay*, 156–62.

16. *Cat*, 114.

17. David A. Miller, *The Novel and the Police*, 205–6.

18. Miller, *The Novel and the Police*, 207; see Eve Kosofsky Sedgwick, *Epistemology of the Closet*, ch. 1.

19. Savran, *Communists, Cowboys, and Queers*, 115.

20. Tennessee Williams, *Memoirs*, 15–16, 218–19, 245; Donald Spoto, *The Kindness of Strangers*, 215.

21. See Jeffrey Weeks, *Sex, Politics and Society*, 2nd edn, 105.

22. Savran, *Communists, Cowboys, and Queers*, 81, 145.

23. See Henri Arvon, *Marxist Esthetics*; Terry Eagleton, *Marxism and Literary Criticism*; Colin MacCabe, "Realism and the Cinema: Notes on Some Brechtian Theses", MacCabe, "Theory and Film: Principles of Realism and Pleasure."

24. Quoted by Savran, *Communists, Cowboys, and Queers*, 79.

25. Marion Magid, "The Innocence of Tennessee Williams," 73–74.

26. Sacvan Bercovitch, *The American Jeremiad*, 179–80, and ch. 6.

27. Kate Davy, "Reading Past the Heterosexual Imperative," 158, 162. See Davy, "Constructing the Spectator: Reception, Context and Address in Lesbian Performance"; Sue-Ellen Case, "Towards a Butch-Femme Aesthetic"; Jill Dolan, "Breaking the Code: Musings on Lesbian Sexuality and the Performer."

28. Sue-Ellen Case's argument on *Dress Suits* is reported in Lynda Hart, "Identity and Seduction: Lesbians in the Mainstream," 120.

29. Lynda Hart, "Identity and Seduction: Lesbians in the Mainstream," 121–22, 124.

30. Teresa de Lauretis, "Sexual Indifference and Lesbian Representation," 159.

31. Jonathan Dollimore and Alan Sinfield, eds., *Political Shakespeare*, 13. See Dollimore and Sinfield, "Culture and Textuality: Debating Cultural Materialism"; Sinfield, "Private Lives/Public Theatre: Noel Coward and the Politics of Homosexual Representation."

32. Miller, *The Novel and the Police*, 206; Nicholas de Jongh, *Not in Front of the Audience*, 77. For Williams's response to Kerr, see St Just, *Five O'Clock Angel*, 108–10.

33. Williams, *Cat*, 168, 214–15; see Brenda Murphy, *Tennessee Williams and Elia Kazan*, 103–7.

34. Gene D. Phillips, *The Films of Tennessee Williams*, 144–47.

35. Maurice Yacowar, *Tennessee Williams and Film*, 43.

36. Yacowar, *Tennessee Williams and Film*, 43.

37. Robert Brustein, *Seasons of Discontent*, 83–93. Brustein's case is accepted by Sarotte, *Like a Brother*, ch. 9.

38. Stanley Kauffmann, *Persons of the Drama*, 291–93. See Clum, *Acting Gay*, 175–76; Michael Bronski, *Culture Clash*, 124–28; Kaier Curtin, *"We Can Always Call Them Bulgarians"*, 320–26.

39. Allan Bérubé, foreword to Steven Zeeland, *Barrack Buddies and Soldier Lovers*, x.

40. See Anna Marie Smith, "Resisting the Erasure of Lesbian Sexuality"; Cherry Smyth, *Lesbians Talk Queer Notions*, 22–24, 26–27.

41. David T. Evans, *Sexual Citizenship*, 50–54.

42. Dennis Altman, *Homosexual: Oppression and Liberation*, 219.

43. Hans Mayer, *Outsiders*, 18.

44. Sedgwick, *Epistemology*, 85.

45. See Smith, "Resisting the Erasure"; Vicki Carter, "Abseil Makes the Heart Grow Fonder: Lesbian and Gay Campaigning Tactics and Section 28"; Bérubé, foreword to Zeeland, *Barrack Buddies and Soldier Lovers*, xi.

Notes to Chapter 4

1. W.H. Auden, *Collected Shorter Poems 1927–1957*, 315–17.

2. Alan Sinfield, *Literature, Politics and Culture in Postwar Britain*, 67–68; Laurence Lerner, "Unwriting Literature," 796, 812. My argument here draws on Sinfield, "'Reading Extraneously': A Reply to Laurence Lerner."

3. Ekbert Faas, *Young Robert Duncan*, 151–52, 154.

4. M.L. Rosenthal, *The New Poets*, 174, 183. See Bergman, *Gaiety Transfigured*, 107–8.

5. Laurence Lerner, "A Response to Alan Sinfield," 216.

6. F.O. Matthieson, *American Renaissance*, 535–36. See Jonathan Arac, "F.O. Matthiessen: Authorizing the American Renaissance"; Michael Cadden, "Engendering F.O.M.: The Private Life of *American Renaissance*"; David Bergman, *Gaiety Transfigured*, ch. 5.

7. Lerner, "Unwriting Literature," 803.

8. W.H. Auden, *Forewords and Afterwords*, 450–58, 336.

9. Faas, *Young Robert Duncan*, 153. See Jonathan Dollimore, *Sexual Dissidence*, 47.

10. See Angela Weir and Elizabeth Wilson, "The Greyhound Bus Station in

the Evolution of Lesbian Popular Culture"; Gabriele Griffin, ed., *Outwrite: Lesbianism and Popular Culture.*

11. Neil Bartlett, *Who Was That Man?*, 33–34. See Eve Kosofsky Sedgwick, *Epistemology of the Closet*, 48–54.

12. Alan Sinfield, "Private Lives/Public Theatre: Noel Coward and the Politics of Homosexual Representation."

13. Annabel Patterson, *Censorship and Interpretation*, 7, 11.

14. Rich, "Split at the Root," 232.

15. Janice A. Radway, *Reading the Romance*, U.K. edn, 8. See Dave Morley, *The Nationwide Audience*; Tony Bennett and Janet Woollacott, *Bond and Beyond*, 60–69, 260–69.

16. Laurence Lerner, "A Response to Alan Sinfield," 214–16.

17. See Teresa de Lauretis, "Sexual Indifference and Lesbian Representation," 169; Sally Munt, *New Lesbian Criticism*, xiii; also Mark Finch, "Sex and Address in 'Dynasty'."

18. Barbara Bradby, "Lesbians and Popular Music: Does It Matter Who Is Singing?" 170–71.

19. Antonio Gramsci, *Selections from the Prison Notebooks*, 324.

20. Frank Parkin, *Class, Inequality and Political Order*, ch. 3; Raymond Williams, "Base and Superstructure in Marxist Cultural Theory," in Williams, *Problems in Materialism and Culture*; Williams, *Culture*, 70–85; Stuart Hall, "Encoding and Decoding." See also Christine Gledhill, "Pleasurable Negotiations."

21. Ann Rosalind Jones, *The Currency of Eros*, 1–10.

22. See Angela McRobbie, "Settling Accounts with Subcultures," also in McRobbie, *Feminism and Youth Culture*; Simon Frith and Angela McRobbie, "Rock and Sexuality"; Angela McRobbie and Jenny Garber, "Girls and Subcultures."

23. Tania Modleski, *Feminism Without Women*, 42–43, and 38–45.

24. Radway, *Reading the Romance*, 9. See Judith Newton and Deborah Rosenfelt, "Introduction: Toward a Materialist-Feminist Criticism"; Ann Rosalind Jones, "Writing the Body: Toward an Understanding of *l'écriture féminine*"; Kadiatu G. Kanneh, "Sisters Under the Skin: a Politics of Heterosexuality."

25. De Lauretis, "Sexual Indifference and Lesbian Representation," 170; Lorde, *Zami*, 203.

26. Sedgwick, *Epistemology*, 85; see 84–90.

27. Lorde, *Zami*, 15, 176, 253. See Anna Wilson, "Audre Lorde and the African-American Tradition: When the Family Is Not Enough."

28. Adrienne Rich, "Compulsory Heterosexuality and Lesbian Existence."

29. LeVay talks with his father in Woodfall Films, *Born That Way?* See also Simon LeVay, *The Sexual Brain*.

30. Robert Pool, "Evidence for Homosexuality Gene"; *Independent*, July 16, 1993.

31. Simon Watney, "The Banality of Gender," 18–19.

32. Jeffrey Weeks, *Against Nature*, 65–66.

33. Diana Fuss, *Essentially Speaking*, 107–8.

34. Pool, "Evidence for Homosexuality Gene," 292.

35. Sue George, *Women and Bisexuality*, 169–81. See Joseph Bristow, "Being Gay: Politics, Identity, Pleasure," 61–68.

36. George, *Women and Bisexuality*, 164.

37. Lee Edelman, "Redeeming the Phallus: Wallace Stevens, Frank Lentricchia, and the Politics of (Hetero)Sexuality," 37.

38. Stanley Fish, "Commentary: The Young and the Restless," 314.

39. Ed Cohen, "Are We (Not) What We Are Becoming? 'Gay' 'Identity,' 'Gay Studies,' and the Disciplining of Knowledge," 161.

40. Hazel V. Carby, *Reconstructing Womanhood*, 15–16; Barbara Ehrenreich, "The Professional-Managerial Class Revisited," 175–77.

41. Walter Benjamin, *Illuminations*, 258.

42. Derek Cohen and Richard Dyer, "The Politics of Gay Culture," 177.

43. Thomas Piontek, "Unsafe Representations: Cultural Criticism in the Age of AIDS," 137. See Jan Zita Grover, "AIDS, Keywords, and Cultural Work"; Stuart Hall, "Cultural Studies and its Theoretical Legacies"; Cornel West, "The Postmodern Crisis of the Black Intellectuals."

44. Fish, "Commentary," in Veeser, 314, 316. Cf. Sinfield, *Literature, Politics and Culture*, 271–74, 300–4; Sinfield, *Faultlines*, 279–302.

45. Antonio Gramsci, *Selections from the Prison Notebooks*, 6–7, 10.

46. Michel Foucault, *Power/Knowledge*, 126–33. See Stuart Hall, "Cultural Studies and Its Theoretical Legacies," 280–81; Eve Tavor Bannet, *Structuralism and the Logic of Dissent*, 168–83.

47. Edward Said, "American Intellectuals and Middle East Politics," 141.

48. Radway, *Reading the Romance*, 17–18; see Angela McRobbie, "The Politics of Feminist Research."

49. West, "The Postmodern Crisis," 695.

50. bell hooks, *Yearning*, 30.

51. Piontek, "Unsafe Representations," 132.

52. Carby, *Reconstructing Womanhood*, 163–66.

53. Thom Gunn, "Interview: Thom Gunn at Sixty."

54. Thom Gunn, *The Man with Night Sweats*, 73.

55. Camille Paglia, "Junk Bonds and Corporate Raiders: Academe in the Hour of the Wolf," 182, 206.

56. Michael Bronski, *Culture Clash*, 7.

57. Roth, *Operation Shylock*, 157.

58. Wilson, "Audre Lorde and the African-American Tradition," 86–87, 90.

59. Dollimore, *Sexual Dissidence*, 287.

60. *Western Morning News*, February 8, 1992; *Independent on Sunday*, February 2, 1992; *Weekend Telegraph*, March 28, 1992.

61. *Observer*, February 9, 1992; *Independent*, February 15, 1992; *Economist*, February 22, 1992.

62. Hilary Hinds, "*Oranges Are Not the Only Fruit*: Reaching Audiences Other Lesbian Texts Cannot Reach," 167, 162. See Lynda Hart, "Identity and Seduction: Lesbians in the Mainstream."

63. Benjamin, *Illuminations*, 258; Jean Genet, "Introduction," 22.

64. Kevin Porter and Jeffrey Weeks, eds., *Between the Acts*, 29.

Texts Cited

Adelman, Janet. *Suffocating Mothers*. New York: Routledge, 1992.

Altman, Dennis. *Homosexual: Oppression and Liberation*. Sidney and London: Angus and Robertson, 1972.

Althusser, Louis. *Lenin and Philosophy and Other Essays*. Trans. Ben Brewster. London: New Left Books, 1971.

Arac, Jonathan. "F.O. Matthiessen: Authorizing the American Renaissance." In *The American Renaissance Reconsidered*, ed. Walter Benn Michaels and Donald E. Pease.

Arvon, Henri. *Marxist Esthetics*. Trans. Helen R. Lane. Ithaca, NY: Cornell University Press, 1973.

Auden, W.H. *The Dyer's Hand*. London: Faber, 1963.

Auden, W.H. *Forewords and Afterwords*. Ed. Edward Mendelson. London: Faber, 1973.

Auden, W.H. *Collected Shorter Poems 1927–1957*. London: Faber and Faber, 1966.

Austen, Alfred. "The Poetry of the Period." In *The Victorian Poet*, ed. Joseph Bristow.

Babbitt, Irving. *Literature and the American College*. Boston: Houghton Mifflin, 1908.

Barber, C.L. *Shakespeare's Festive Comedy*. Princeton, NJ: Princeton University Press, 1972.

Bartlett, Neil. *Who Was That Man?* London: Serpent's Tale, 1988.

Benjamin, Walter. *Illuminations*. Ed. Hannah Arendt. Trans. Harry Zohn. Glasgow: Fontana/Collins, 1973.

Bennett, Tony. *Formalism and Marxism*. London: Methuen, 1979.

Bennett, Tony and Janet Woollacott. *Bond and Beyond*. London: Macmillan, 1987.

Bennett, William. "To Reclaim a Legacy." *American Education* 21 (1985): 4–15.

Bercovitch, Sacvan. *The American Jeremiad*. Madison: University of Wisconsin Press, 1978.

Bergman, David. *Gaiety Transfigured*. Madison: University of Wisconsin Press, 1991.

Bérubé, Allan. *Coming Out Under Fire*. New York: Plume, 1991.

Bieber, Irving, ed. *Homosexuality: A Psychoanalytic Study*. New York: Vintage Books, 1962.

Bloom, Alexander. *Prodigal Sons*. New York: Oxford University Press, 1986.

Bloom, Allan. *The Closing of the American Mind*. New York: Simon and Schuster, 1987.

Bloom, Allan with Harry V. Jaffa. *Shakespeare's Politics*. Chicago: University of Chicago Press, Midway Reprint, 1986.

Boone, Joseph A. and Michael Cadden, eds. *Engendering Men*. New York: Routledge, 1990.

Bradby, Barbara. "Lesbians and Popular Music: Does It Matter Who Is Singing?" In *Outwrite*, ed. Gabriele Griffin.

Bray, Alan. "Homosexuality and the Signs of Male Friendship in Elizabethan England." *History Workshop* 29 (1990): 1–19.

———. *Homosexuality in Renaissance England*. London: Gay Men's Press, 1982.

Bristow, Joseph. "Being Gay: Politics, Identity, Pleasure." *New Formations* 9 (1989): 61–81.

———, ed. *The Victorian Poet: Poetics and Persona*. London: Croom Helm, 1987.

Bronski, Michael. *Culture Clash*. Boston: South End Press, 1984.

Brustein, Robert. *Seasons of Discontent*. London: Cape, 1966.

Bush, Douglas. *Mythology and the Renaissance Tradition*. Minneapolis: University of Minnesota Press, 1932.

Bychowski, Gustav. "The Ego of Homosexuals." *International Journal of Psychoanalysis* 26 (1945): 125.

Cadden, Michael. "Engendering F.O.M.: The Private Life of *American Renaissance*." In *Engendering Men*, ed. Joseph A. Boone and Michael Cadden.

Carby, Hazel V. *Reconstructing Womanhood*. New York: Oxford University Press, 1987.

Carter, Vicki. "Abseil Makes the Heart Grow Fonder: Lesbian and Gay Campaigning Tactics and Section 28." In *Modern Homosexualities*, ed. Ken Plummer.

Case, Sue-Ellen. "Towards a Butch-Femme Aesthetic." *Discourse* 11 (1988–89): 55–73.

Clum, John M. *Acting Gay*. New York: Columbia University Press, 1992.

Cohen, Derek and Richard Dyer. "The Politics of Gay Culture." In *Homosexuality: Power and Politics*, ed. Gay Left Collective.

Cohen, Ed. "Are We Not What We Are Becoming? 'Gay' 'Identity,' 'Gay Studies,' and the Disciplining of Knowledge." In *Engendering Men*, ed. Joseph A. Boone and Michael Cadden.

Cohen, Walter. "Political Criticism of Shakespeare." In *Shakespeare Reproduced*, ed. Jean E. Howard and Marion F. O'Connor.

Curtin, Kaier. *"We Can Always Call Them Bulgarians."* Boston: Alyson, 1987.

Davy, Kate. "Constructing the Spectator: Reception, Context and Address in Lesbian Performance." *Performing Arts Journal* 10, 2 (1986): 43–52.

———. "From *Lady Dick* to Ladylike: The Work of Holly Hughes. In *Acting Out*, ed. Lynda Hart and Peggy Phelan.

———. "Reading Past the Heterosexual Imperative." *TDR: The Drama Review* 33 (1989): 153–70.

De Jongh, Nicholas. *Not in Front of the Audience*. London: Routledge, 1992.

De Lauretis, Teresa. "Sexual Indifference and Lesbian Representation." *Theatre Journal* 40 (1988): 155–77.

D'Emilio, John. *Making Trouble*. New York: Routledge, 1992.

Dolan, Jill. "Breaking the Code: Musings on Lesbian Sexuality and the Performer." *Modern Drama* 32 (1989): 146–58.

Dollimore, Jonathan. *Sexual Dissidence*. Oxford: Clarendon Press, 1991.

Dollimore, Jonathan and Alan Sinfield, "Culture and Textuality: Debating Cultural Materialism." *Textual Practice* 4 (1990): 91–100.

———, eds. *Political Shakespeare*. Manchester: Manchester University Press, 1985.

Douglas, Ann. *The Feminization of American Culture*. New York: Avon Books, 1978.

Eagleton, Terry. *Literary Theory: An Introduction*. Oxford: Blackwell, 1983.

———. *Marxism and Literary Criticism*. London: Methuen, 1976.

———. *William Shakespeare*. Oxford: Blackwell, 1986.

Edelman, Lee. "Redeeming the Phallus: Wallace Stevens, Frank Lentricchia, and the Politics of (Hetero)Sexuality." In *Engendering Men*, ed. Joseph A. Boone and Michael Cadden.

———. "Tearooms and Sympathy, or, The Epistemology of the Water Closet." In *Nationalisms and Sexualities*, ed. Andrew Parker et al.

Ehrenreich, Barbara. *The Hearts of Men*. London: Pluto, 1983.

———. "The Professional-Managerial Class Revisited." In *Intellectuals: Aesthetics, Politics, Academics*, ed. Bruce Robbins.

Ellis, Havelock. *Studies in the Psychology of Sex*. Vol 2 part 2, *Sexual Inversion*, 1900; New York: Random House, 1936.

Evans, David T. *Sexual Citizenship*. London: Routledge, 1993.

Faas, Ekbert. *Young Robert Duncan*. Santa Barbara, CA: Black Sparrow Press, 1983.

Fiedler, Leslie. *Waiting for the End*. Harmondsworth: Penguin, 1967.

Finch, Mark. "Sex and Address in 'Dynasty'." *Screen* 27, 6 (1986): 24–42.

Fish, Stanley. "Commentary: The Young and the Restless." In *The New Historicism*, ed. H. Aram Veeser.

Foucault, Michel. *The History of Sexuality, vol. 1, An Introduction*. Trans. Robert Hurley. New York: Vintage Books, 1978.

———. *Power/Knowledge*. Ed. Colin Gordon. Brighton: Harvester, 1980.

Freud, Sigmund. *Standard Edition of the Complete Psychological Works*. Ed. James Strachey, vol. 23. London: Hogarth, 1964.

Frith, Simon and Angela McRobbie. "Rock and Sexuality." *Screen Education* 29 (Winter 1978/9): 3–19.

Fuss, Diana. *Essentially Speaking*. New York: Routledge, 1989.

Gay Left Collective, eds. *Homosexuality: Power and Politics*. London: Allison and Busby, 1980.

Gelpi, Barbara Charlesworth and Albert Gelpi, eds. *Adrienne Rich's Poetry and Prose*. New York: Norton, 1993.

Genet, Jean. "Introduction" to George Jackson, *Soledad Brother*. Harmondsworth: Penguin, 1971.

George, Sue. *Women and Bisexuality*. London: Scarlet Press, 1993.

Gilbert, Sandra M. and Susan Gubar. *No Man's Land*. Vol. 1, *The War of the Words*. New Haven, CT and London: Yale University Press, 1988.

Ginsberg, Allen. *"Howl" and Other Poems*. San Francisco: City Lights, 1959.

Gledhill, Christine. "Pleasurable Negotiations." In *Female Spectators*, ed. E. Deidre Pribram.

Goldberg, Jonathan. *Sodometries*. Stanford, CA: Stanford University Press, 1992.

Gramsci, Antonio. *Selections from the Prison Notebooks*. Trans. Quintin Hoare and Geoffrey Nowell Smith. London: Lawrence and Wishart, 1971.

Greenberg, David F. *The Construction of Homosexuality*. Chicago: University of Chicago Press, 1988.

Griffin, Gabriele, ed. *Outwrite: Lesbianism and Popular Culture*. London: Pluto, 1993.

———. *Heavenly Love*. Manchester: Manchester University Press, 1993.

Gross, John. *Shylock*. London: Chatto, 1992.

Grossberg, Lawrence, Cary Nelson and Paula A. Treichler, eds., *Cultural Studies*. New York: Routledge, 1992.

Grover, Jan Zita. "AIDS, Keywords, and Cultural Work." In *Cultural Studies*, ed. Lawrence Grossberg et al.

Gunn, Thom. "Interview: Thom Gunn at Sixty." *Gay Times* 131 (August 1989): 26–29. Reprinted, slightly extended: "Thom Gunn in San Francisco: An Interview." *Critical Survey* 2 (1990): 223–30.

———. *The Man with Night Sweats*. London: Faber, 1992.

Hall, Stuart. "Cultural Studies and Its Theoretical Legacies." In *Cultural Studies*, ed. Lawrence Grossberg et al.

———. "Encoding and Decoding." In *Culture, Media, Language*, ed. Stuart Hall et al.

Hall, Stuart, Dorothy Hobson, Andrew Lowe, and Paul Willis, eds. *Culture, Media, Language*. London: Hutchinson, 1980.

Hall, Stuart and Tony Jefferson, eds. *Resistance Through Rituals*. London: Hutchinson and Centre for Contemporary Cultural Studies, 1976.

Halperin, David M. *One Hundred Years of Homosexuality*. New York: Routledge, 1990.

Hart, Lynda. "Identity and Seduction: Lesbians in the Mainstream." In *Acting Out*, ed. Lynda Hart and Peggy Phelan.

Hart, Lynda and Peggy Phelan, eds. *Acting Out*. Ann Arbor: University of Michigan Press, 1993.

Hawkes, Terence. *Meaning by Shakespeare*. London: Routledge, 1992.

Hinds, Hilary. "*Oranges Are Not the Only Fruit*: Reaching Audiences Other Lesbian Texts Cannot Reach." In *New Lesbian Criticism*, ed. Sally Munt.

Hirsch, Jr., E.D. *Cultural Literacy*. Boston: Houghton Mifflin, 1987.

Holderness, Graham, ed. *The Shakespeare Myth*. Manchester University Press, 1988.

hooks, bell. *Yearning*. London: Turnaround, 1991.

Howard, Jean E. "Crossdressing, the Theatre and Gender Struggle in Early Modern England." *Shakespeare Quarterly* 39 (1988): 418–40.

Howard, Jean E. and Marion F. O'Connor. "Introduction." In *Shakespeare Reproduced*, ed. Jean E. Howard and Marion F. O'Connor.

———, eds. *Shakespeare Reproduced*. New York and London: Methuen, 1987.

Jacoby, Russell. *The Last Intellectuals*. New York: Basic Books, 1987.

Jameson, Fredric. *Marxism and Form*. Princeton, NJ: Princeton University Press, 1971.

Jones, Ann Rosalind. *The Currency of Eros*. Bloomington and Indianapolis: Indiana University Press, 1990.

———. "Writing the Body: Toward an Understanding of *l'écriture féminine*." In *Feminist Criticism and Social Change*, ed. Judith Newton and Deborah Rosenfelt.

Kahn, Coppélia. *Man's Estate*. Berkeley: University of California Press, 1981.

Kanneh, Kadiatu G. "Sisters Under the Skin: A Politics of Heterosexuality." *Feminism and Psychology*, Special Issue on Heterosexuality 2 (1992): 432–33.

Kardiner, Abram. "The Flight from Masculinity." In *The Problem of Homosexuality in Modern Society*, ed. Hendrik M. Ruitenbeek.

Kauffmann, Stanley. *Persons of the Drama*. New York: Harper and Row, 1976.

Kelsall, Malcolm, Martin Coyle, Peter Garside, and John Peck, eds. *Encyclopedia of Literature and Criticism*. London: Routledge, 1990.

Kingsley, Charles. *Literary and General Essays*. London: Macmillan, 1890.

Klingenstein, Susanne. *Jews in the American Academy 1900–1940*. New Haven, CT: Yale University Press, 1991.

Laclau, Ernesto and Chantal Mouffe. *Hegemony and Socialist Strategy*. London: Verso, 1985.

Leavis, F.R. *Revaluation*. London: Chatto, 1936.

Lerner, Laurence. "A Response to Alan Sinfield." *New Literary History* 23 (1992): 214–16.

———. "Unwriting Literature." *New Literary History*, 22 (1991): 795–815.

LeVay, Simon. *The Sexual Brain*. Cambridge, MA: MIT Press, 1993.

Levine, Laura. "Men in Women's Clothing: Antitheatricality and Effeminization from 1579 to 1642." *Criticism* 28 (1986): 121–43.

Lewes, Kenneth. *The Psychoanalytic Theory of Male Homosexuality*. London: Quartet, 1989.

Liu, Alan. "The Power of Formalism: The New Historicism." *English Literary History* 56 (1989): 721–77.

Loomba, Ania. *Gender, Race, Renaissance Drama*. Manchester: Manchester University Press, 1989.

Lorde, Audre. *Zami: A New Spelling of My Name*. New York: Crossing Press, 1983.

MacCabe, Colin. "Realism and the Cinema: Notes on Some Brechtian Theses." *Screen* 15, 2 (1974): 7–27.

———. "Theory and Film: Principles of Realism and Pleasure." *Screen* 17, 3 (1976): 7–27.

Macherey, Pierre. *A Theory of Literary Production*. Trans. Geoffrey Wall. London: Routledge, 1978.

Macherey, Pierre and Etienne Balibar. "Literature as an Ideological Form: Some Marxist Propositions." *Oxford Literary Review* 3 (1978): 4–12.

Magid, Marion. "The Innocence of Tennessee Williams." In *Twentieth Century Interpretations of "A Streetcar Named Desire"*, ed. Jordan Y. Miller.

Mailer, Norman. *Advertisements for Myself*. London: Panther, 1968.

Marcuse, Herbert. *An Essay on Liberation*. Harmondsworth: Penguin, 1972.

Marlowe, Christopher. *The Plays of Christopher Marlowe*. Ed. Roma Gill. Oxford: Oxford University Press, 1971.

Marx, Karl. *Grundrisse*. Trans. Martin Nicolaus. Harmondsworth: Penguin, 1973.

Matthieson, F.O. *American Renaissance*. New York: Oxford University Press, 1941.

Mayer, Hans. *Outsiders*. Trans. Denis M. Sweet. Cambridge, MA.: MIT Press, 1982.

McRobbie, Angela. *Feminism and Youth Culture*. Basingstoke: Macmillan, 1991.

————. "Settling Accounts with Subcultures." *Screen Education* 24 (Spring 1990): 37–49. Also in McRobbie, *Feminism and Youth Culture*.

McRobbie, Angela and Jenny Garber. "Girls and Subcultures." In *Resistance Through Rituals*, ed. Stuart Hall and Tony Jefferson.

Michaels, Walter Benn and Donald E. Pease, eds. *The American Renaissance Reconsidered*. Baltimore: Johns Hopkins University Press, 1985.

Miller, Arthur. *A View from the Bridge; All My Sons, All My Sons*. Harmondsworth: Penguin, 1961.

Miller, David A. *The Novel and the Police*. Berkeley: University of California Press, 1988.

Miller, Jordan Y., ed. *Twentieth Century Interpretations of "A Streetcar Named Desire."* Englewood Cliffs, NJ: Prentice-Hall, 1971.

Milton, John. *Poetical Works*. Ed. Douglas Bush. Oxford University Press, 1969.

Modleski, Tania. *Feminism Without Women*. New York: Routledge, 1991.

Montrose, Louis. "Professing the Renaissance: The Poetics and Politics of Culture." In *The New Historicism*, ed. Aram H. Veeser.

Morley, Dave. *The Nationwide Audience*. London: British Film Institute, 1980.

Munt, Sally, ed. *New Lesbian Criticism*. Hemel Hempstead: Harvester Wheatsheaf, 1992.

Murphy, Brenda. *Tennessee Williams and Elia Kazan*. Cambridge University Press, 1992.

Murray, Stephen O. "The 'Underdevelopment' of Modern/Gay Homosexuality in Mesoamerica." In *Modern Homosexualities*, ed. Ken Plummer.

Newton, Judith and Deborah Rosenfelt, eds. *Feminist Criticism and Social Change*. New York: Methuen, 1985.

O'Connor, Garry. *William Shakespeare: A Life*. London: Hodder and Stoughton, 1991.

Orgel, Stephen. "Nobody's Perfect: Or Why Did the English Stage Take Boys for Women?" *South Atlantic Quarterly* 88 (1989): 7–29.

Ovesey, Lionel. "The Homosexual Conflict: An Adaptational Analysis." In *The Problem of Homosexuality in Modern Society*, ed. Hendrik M. Ruitenbeek.

Paglia, Camille. "Junk Bonds and Corporate Raiders: Academe in the Hour of the Wolf." *Arion* 3rd series, 1 (Spring 1991): 139–212.

Parker, Andrew, Mary Russo, Doris Sommer, and Patricia Yaeger, eds., *Nationalisms and Sexualities*. New York: Routledge, 1992.

Parkin, Frank. *Class, Inequality and Political Order*. London: Paladin, 1972.

Partridge, Eric. *Shakespeare's Bawdy*. New York: Dutton, 1948.

Patterson, Annabel. *Censorship and Interpretation*. Madison: University of Wisconsin Press, 1984.

Pease, Donald. *"Moby Dick* and the Cold War." In *The American Renaissance Reconsidered*, ed. W.B. Michaels and D.E. Pease.

Phillips, Gene D. *The Films of Tennessee Williams*. Philadelphia: Art Alliance Press, 1980.

Piontek, Thomas. "Unsafe Representations: Cultural Criticism in the Age of AIDS." *Discourse* 15 (1992): 128–53.

Plummer, Ken, ed. *Modern Homosexualities*. London: Routledge, 1992.

Pool, Robert. "Evidence for Homosexuality Gene." *Science* 261, 265–396 (July 16, 1993): 291–92.

Poovey, Mary. *Uneven Developments*. London: Virago, 1989.

Porter, Kevin and Jeffrey Weeks, eds. *Between the Acts*. London: Routledge, 1991.

Poulantzas, Nicos. *Political Power and Social Classes*. Trans. Timothy O'Hagan. London: New Left Books, 1973.

Pribram, E. Deidre, ed. *Female Spectators*. London: Verso, 1988.

Radway, Janice A. *Reading the Romance*. London: Verso, 1987.

Ramanathan, Saguna. "Teaching English Literature in Post-colonial India." Paper delivered at the University of Salamanca, 1992.

Rich, Adrienne. *Blood, Bread and Poetry*. New York: Norton, 1986.

———. "Split at the Root: An Essay on Jewish Identity." In *Adrienne Rich's Poetry and Prose*, ed. Barbara Charlesworth Gelpi and Albert Gelpi.

———. "Compulsory Homosexuality and Lesbian Existence." In *Adrienne Rich's Poetry and Prose*, ed. Barbara Charlesworth Gelpi and Albert Gelpi.

Ricks, Christopher. *T.S. Eliot and Prejudice*. London: Faber, 1988.

Robbins, Bruce, ed. *Intellectuals: Aesthetics, Politics, Academics*. Minneapolis: University of Minnesota Press, 1990.

Robinson, Lillian S. *Sex, Class, and Culture*. New York and London: Methuen, 1986.

Rosenthal, M.L. *The New Poets*. New York: Oxford University Press, 1967.

Roth, Philip. *Operation Shylock*. New York: Simon and Schuster, 1993.

Ruitenbeek, Hendrik M., ed. *The Problem of Homosexuality in Modern Society*. New York: Dutton, 1963.

Said, Edward. "American Intellectuals and Middle East Politics." In *Intellectuals: Aesthetics, Politics, Academics*, ed. Bruce Robbins.

Sarotte, Georges-Michel. *Like a Brother, Like a Lover*. Trans. Richard Miller. New York: Anchor/Doubleday, 1978.

Savran, David. *Communists, Cowboys, and Queers*. Minneapolis: University of Minnesota Press, 1992.

Sedgwick, Eve Kosofsky. *Between Men*. New York: Columbia University Press, 1985.

———. *Epistemology of the Closet*. Hemel Hempstead: Harvester Wheatsheaf, 1991.

Shakespeare, William. *Antony and Cleopatra*. Ed. M.R. Ridley. New Arden edn. London: Methuen, 1962.

———. *Coriolanus*. Ed. Philip Brockbank. New Arden edn. London: Methuen, 1976.

———. *The Poems*. Ed. F.T. Prince. London: Methuen, 1960.

———. *The Poems*. New Variorum Edition, ed. Hyder Edward Rollins. Philadelphia: J.B. Lippincott, 1938.

———. *Romeo and Juliet*. Ed. Brian Gibbons. New Arden edn. London and New York: Methuen, 1980.

———. *Troilus and Cressida*. Ed. Kenneth Palmer. New Arden edn. London and New York: Methuen, 1982.

Shepherd, Simon. "Shakespeare's Private Drawer: Shakespeare and Homosexuality." In *The Shakespeare Myth*, ed. Graham Holderness.

Showalter, Elaine, ed. *The New Feminist Criticism*. London: Virago, 1986.

———. "Toward a Feminist Poetics." In *The New Feminist Criticism*, ed. Elaine Showalter.

Sinfield, Alan. *Alfred Tennyson*. Oxford: Blackwell, 1986.

———. *Faultlines: Cultural Materialism and the Politics of Dissident Reading*. Berkeley: University of California Press; Oxford: Oxford University Press, 1992.

———. *Literature, Politics and Culture in Postwar Britain*. Oxford: Blackwell; Berkeley: University of California Press, 1989.

———. "Private Lives/Public Theatre: Noel Coward and the Politics of Homosexual Representation." *Representations* 36 (Fall 1991): 43–63.

———. "'Reading Extraneously': A Reply to Laurence Lerner". *New Literary History* 23 (1992): 213–14.

———. *The Wilde Century: Effeminacy, Oscar Wilde and the Queer Moment*. London: Cassell, 1994.

Smith, Anna Marie. "Resisting the Erasure of Lesbian Sexuality." In *Modern Homosexualities*, ed. Ken Plummer.

Smith, Bruce R. *Homosexual Desire in Shakespeare's England*. Chicago: University of Chicago Press, 1991.

Smyth, Cherry. *Lesbians Talk Queer Notions*. London: Scarlet Press, 1992.

Spoto, Donald. *The Kindness of Strangers*. London: Bodley Head, 1985.

St. Just, Maria, ed. *Five O'Clock Angel*. London: Deutsch, 1991.

Stone, Lawrence. *The Family, Sex and Marriage in England 1500–1800*. London: Weidenfeld and Nicolson, 1977.

Summers, Claude, ed. *Homosexuality in Renaissance and Enlightenment England*. New York: Harrington Park, 1992.

Symonds, John Addington. *The Memoirs of John Addington Symonds*. Ed. Phyllis Grosskurth. London: Hutchinson, 1984.

Tapinc, Huseyin. "Masculinity, Femininity and Turkish Male Homosexuality." In *Modern Homosexualities*, ed. Ken Plummer.

Tavor Bannet, Eve. *Structuralism and the Logic of Dissent*. London: Macmillan, 1989.

David Thacker. "Understanding Shylock." (London) *Sunday Times*, June 13, 1993, part 9, 23.

Traub, Valerie. *Desire and Anxiety*. New York: Routledge, 1992.

Van Doren, Mark. *The Private Reader*. New York: Kraus Reprint Co., 1968.

Veeser, H. Aram, ed. *The New Historicism*. New York: Routledge, 1989.

Watney, Simon. "The Banality of Gender." *Oxford Literary Review* 8 (1986): 13–21.

Wayne, Don E. "New Historicism." In *Encyclopedia of Literature and Criticism*, ed. Malcolm Kelsall et al.

———. "Power, Politics and the Shakespearean Text: Recent Criticism in England and the United States." In *Shakespeare Reproduced*, ed. Jean E. Howard and Marion F. O'Connor.

Weeks, Jeffrey. *Against Nature*. London: Rivers Oram, 1991.

———. *Sex, Politics and Society*. 2nd edn. London: Longman, 1989.

Weir, Angela and Elizabeth Wilson. "The Greyhound Bus Station in the Evolution of Lesbian Popular Culture." In *New Lesbian Criticism*, ed. Sally Munt.

Wesker, Arnold. *The Journalists/The Wedding Feast/Shylock*. Harmondsworth: Penguin, 1990.

West, Cornel. "The Postmodern Crisis of the Black Intellectuals." In *Cultural Studies*, ed. Lawrence Grossberg et al.

Williams, Raymond. *Culture*. Glasgow: Fontana, 1981.

———. *Culture and Society 1780–1950*. Harmondsworth: Penguin, 1961.

———. *Marxism and Literature*. Oxford: Oxford University Press, 1977.

———. *Keywords*. London: Croom Helm, 1976.

———. *Problems in Materialism and Culture*. London: New Left Books, 1980.

Williams, Tennessee. *Memoirs*. New York: Bantam, 1976.

———. *The Theatre of Tennessee Williams*. Vol. 3. New York: New Directions, 1971.

———. *The Theatre of Tennessee Williams*. Vol. 4. New York: New Directions, 1972.

Wilson, Anna. "Audre Lorde and the African-American Tradition: When the Family Is Not Enough." In *New Lesbian Criticism*, ed. Sally Munt.

Wolff, Max Joseph. *Shakespeare der Dichter und sein Werk*, vol. 1. Munich: C.H. Beck, 1907.

Wolff, Robert Paul, Barrington Moore, Jr., and Herbert Marcuse. *A Critique of Pure Tolerance*. London: Cape, 1969.

Woodfall Films, *Born That Way?* London: Woodfall Films for Channel Four, 1992.

Woods, Gregory. "Body, Costume, and Desire in Christopher Marlowe." In *Homosexuality in Renaissance and Enlightenment England*, ed. Claude Summers.

Woolf, Virginia. *Three Guineas*. Harmondsworth: Penguin, 1977.

Yacowar, Maurice. *Tennessee Williams and Film*. New York: Frederick Ungar, 1977.

Yaffe, James. *The American Jews*. New York: Random House, 1968.

Zeeland, Steven. *Barrack Buddies and Soldier Lovers*. New York: Harrington Park, 1993.

Index

This book has been set in Linotron Galliard. Galliard was designed for Mergenthaler in 1978 by Matthew Carter. Galliard retains many of the features of a sixteenth-century typeface cut by Robert Granjon but has some modifications that give it a more contemporary look.

Printed on acid-free paper.